THE
OLDER
HORSE

SECOND EDITION

The
OLDER
HORSE

*A Complete Guide
to Care and Conditioning
for Horses 10 and Up*

SECOND EDITION

By
Eleanor M. Kellon, VMD

In fond memory of
"Fran's Billy Bob,"
who showed everyone
that heart and spirit
can overcome the ravages
of age.

Copyright © 1986 by Eleanor M. Kellon, VMD

Second edition 1993

For information address:
Breakthrough Publications, Inc.
310 North Highland Avenue
Ossining, New York 10562

Portions of some chapters were originally published by *The Chronicle of the Horse* and are reprinted here with their permission.

The following products mentioned in this book are Registered in the U.S. Patent and Trademark Office: Arquel (Parke-Davis), Banamine (Syntex), Ben-Gay (Leeming), Betadine (Perdue Frederick), Calf Manna (Carnation), Dipyrone (Med-Tech), Equiproxen (Syntex), Fluvac (Fort Dodge), Horsehage (Hillendale Farm), Pitocin (Parke-Davis), Rhinomune (Norden), and Strongid C (Pfizer).

Library of Congress Catalog Card Number: 93-71630
Book design by Jacques Chazaud
Manufactured in the United States of America

ISBN: 0-914327-50-X

99 98 97   5 4 3

Contents

Preface to Second Edition

Since I wrote the first edition of this book in 1986, we have learned so much more about how to care for and treat the older horse, with improved nutrition, better diagnostic procedures and less stress.

The second edition contains much updated material on vaccination, deworming, nutrition, and breeding. I have expanded many sections to include the latest medical treatments or surgical operations for various problems facing the older horse.

In Chapter 2, I have added a thorough discussion of the new strangles vaccine, and I have discussed the importance of the rabies vaccine, together with the characteristics of rabies in a horse and the various conditions that can be confused with rabies. In addition, I describe the characteristics of Potomac horse fever and give advice on vaccination. With the growing prevalence of Lyme disease, I have provided the latest information on this potentially debilitating disease.

In the area of deworming, I have completely revised my advice on deworming, reflecting the newest approaches to parasite control. Information on new medicine and updated schedules are included.

Perhaps most changes have occurred in our knowledge of nutrition for the older horse. I have listed the increased requirements for protein, calcium, phosphorus, and vitamin C in Chapter 3, and have emphasized the importance of protein supplementation and the role of yeast cultures. The newest addition to processed concentrates is extruded feed. This is illustrated, along with processed feed. I set forth new, complete feed options, and I have extensively revised adequate dietary concentrations.

Chapter 13 on breeding the older horse has been updated to include the newest information on calcium and phosphorus, especially as required by the pregnant older mare. The roles of zinc and copper are expanded upon.

Most important, I have discussed extensively the latest medical treatments or surgical operations that are currently available. Early intervention is the key to avoiding life-threatening situations, especially in older horses who are more susceptible to multiple causes of disease. The advance of laparoscopic surgery is vital, because it can determine more easily what the problem is and help in planning necessary procedures. It is not so invasive and prevents unnecessary surgery. Consequently, many problems can be resolved with much less stress to the horse, and with much lower risk of major complications such as hemorrhage or infection.

Finally, I include in Chapter 11 the exciting research that is being done on treatment and diagnosis of arthritis that could greatly improve the quality of life for older horses. And, in a new section on back pain, I discuss the major advances in joint surgery, particularly anthroscopic diagnosis and treatment.

Acknowledgments

Thanks to the following who offered many wonderful photographs and stories concerning their older horses—Alice Bennett, Park Forest, Illinois; Caroline Berry, Zebulon, North Carolina; CARYN, Wyckoff, New Jersey; Rebecca Crystal, Colcomb, New York; Katy Finegan, Gettysburg, Pennsylvania; Lee and Cynthia Foley, Syracuse, New York; Brooke Gaiser, Sarasota, Florida; Elvia Gignous, Salisbury, Connecticut; Lisa Goldrick, Ridgewood, New Jersey; Bobbi Groover, Wadsworth, Illinois; Michelle Hoffman, Davis, California; Mrs. R. James Hubbard, Cazenovia, New York; Valerie Kalima, Post Falls, Idaho; Audrey Petschek, New Canaan, Connecticut; Judy Sears, Cazenovia, New York; Richard Sears, Sheds, New York; Shenandoah Valley Special Riding Program, Port Republic, Virginia; Thorncroft Equestrian Center, Malvern, Pennsylvania; and Susan Woods, Byfield, Massachusetts—and to *The Chronicle of the Horse,* in which portions of some chapters have appeared previously.

Thanks to Hoffman-LaRoche, Inc. for vitamin and mineral information.

Special thanks to Mr. Richard Wright of Pensfeld Feeds for his assistance in compiling nutritional information.

Special thanks to Cynthia Foley and Dr. Eileen Fatcheric for providing the photographs on pages 119, 122, and 148.

Preface to First Edition

HOUSTON CLASSIC—
The USGPL $25,000 Grand Prix of Houston

". . . Honest Tom not only had the fastest time in the jump-off but rode the fastest clean round on their first trip. . . . a 14-year-old Irish-bred gelding. . .certainly showed he has the experience. . . ."

BUFFALO INTERNATIONAL HORSE SHOW

". . . large pony hunter champion, Jamanda, an aged chestnut mare . . . has won six tri-colors so far this season. . . ."

NATIONAL CUTTING HORSE FINALS—
Parker, Colorado

". . . I leased the 19-year-old Morgan mare named Dee Dee Chocolate. She'd been quite the cutting horse in her younger days. . . . I worked her over the summer and took her to the National Cutting Horse Finals in Parker, Colorado, where she won the championship. I later bought her." (David Trexler)

BRITISH INTERNATIONAL DRESSAGE CHAMPIONSHIPS—
West Sussex

". . . . the Intermediaire II was won by Christopher Bartle on the veteran Wily Trout. . . . Now 17 years old, this horse seems if anything to have improved from last year . . . and looks as if he could continue until he is at least 20. . . ."

The accomplishments of the above horses were all cited in just one issue of *The Chronicle of the Horse*, a weekly equine sporting publication. There are also a large number of aged horses among the ranks of racing horses, including the superstar Standardbred Rambling Willie who recorded earnings of over two million dollars before retiring.

Aged horses are capable of doing much more than babysitting yearlings or beginner students. Their wisdom and experience adds immeasurably to their owners' pleasure as they continue to compete with their younger stablemates or serve to introduce another generation of riders to the wonders of horses.

However, maintaining an older horse in top condition requires modifications in management attuned to their special needs. This book will try to give you the information you need to meet these unique requirements by detailing the problems associated with aging and how you can spot them and showing how to maximize the health, happiness, and performance of the aged horse from his active years through retirement.

PART I

Purchase, Care, and Conditioning

1

Purchasing an Older Horse

T he search for that special horse is fun and exciting. It can also be exhausting, time-consuming, and expensive. When you do finally locate a horse with the right "chemistry" and a price to match, as a wise buyer you should make every effort to determine if the horse is truly suitable.

For most people, prepurchase scrutiny is limited to a veterinary examination (often less than complete), a few minutes on the horse's back, and whatever information can be garnered from the sales pitch. This method, however, leaves much room for improvement. (For information on purchasing broodmares, see Chapter 13, "Breeding the Older Horse.")

The veterinary examination is a key element and will be discussed in detail later. Your veterinarian will examine the horse for lameness and medical illnesses and can help you decide if tests such as X-rays are necessary. Suffice it to say here that cutting corners on the veterinary examination could ultimately cost you many times more than the fees you save, particularly with an older horse that is more likely to have problems.

TRYING OUT THE HORSE

Very few people would buy a horse without riding him first, but this contact is usually too brief to be of much value. In addition, the horse is frequently shown by a professional who knows him well and has worked out the kinks before you arrive.

If at all possible, try to get the horse on trial for a few days before you buy. Failing this, make sure you ride the horse at least twice and under different conditions. For example, if the first trial was in midafternoon, in a ring, and after the seller had put the horse through his paces, return early in the morning to hack the horse cross-country (or at least in a field) and request that he not be ridden, longed, or turned out before you ride. An exception to the turnout requirement might be made for a horse that is normally kept turned out—although it could be very useful to see if the horse becomes stiff or very unmanageable when confined even over-night, particularly if your management of him will include stabling. By riding the horse twice you increase your chances of detecting any lameness or behavior problem and generally get to know the animal better.

It is a mistake to assume a horse will be "push-button" for you simply because someone else has had extensive success with him in the past. It takes time to develop that kind of rapport, and some horse/rider combinations will never work out. An older horse is usually very set in his ways. While he may be more tolerant of a rider's mistakes, or at least not unduly flustered by them, he may very well be reluctant to take direction if your ideas of how things should be done differ greatly from those he has grown to accept. If you cannot get a satisfactory response from the horse, even with the advice of his regular rider and trainer, it is best to look elsewhere rather than hope to reschool him. There are exceptions of course, but since one of the great appeals of the older horse is experience, it is far better to find one whose accumulated philosophies are compatible with your own.

Bad Habits

You should also be aware that the horse may come with a set of similarly deep-rooted idiosyncrasies or vices. He may buck if you use a web girth, throw himself down in streams, or try to destroy the trailer at every red light. Make it a point to observe firsthand as many things about the horse as you can. Be in the barn when he is tacked up, observe him on pasture, watch him at shows or in the hunt field. Most importantly, ask a lot of questions.

Inquire specifically if he kicks, bites, rears, hauls poorly, breaks out of the pasture, cribs, eats fencing, destroys his blankets, rushes through doorways, hates dogs, has a morbid fear of cows or mailboxes—or any-thing else you particularly want to avoid! The seller is unlikely to volun-teer such information and cannot really be accused later of misrepre-senting the horse unless specific inquiries were made. Be very certain you can live with any bad habits or quirks an older horse has since any number of attempts have probably already been made to eliminate them.

LEARNING THE HORSE'S HISTORY

There are several other key pieces of information you should obtain before buying a horse. These include past and present activity levels, illnesses and/or lamenesses, routine health care and diet, and shoeing requirements.

Past and Present Activity Levels

An aged horse's performance history may include numerous championships or years of brilliant performance at the activity you desire of him, but this alone has little or no bearing on his present usefulness. You need to assess his present ability to perform at the level you desire. Regular exercise is vitally important to maintain an older horse's muscular, cardiovascular, and joint fitness. If he loses considerable body condition you may never be able to restore him to his previous level of activity or proficiency.

It is a good rule of thumb to be extremely cautious about buying an older horse that is not currently performing at a level equal to or greater than what you will require and *never* to buy a horse just coming off turnout. It is virtually impossible to predict if a horse that has been turned out will hold up to training; even the veterinary examination is of little help here if you will require a drastic change in his activity level.

Medical History and Diet

A horse's past management is also of vital importance. The vaccination history will allow you to plan for immediate administration of necessary boosters, if any, and to appropriately schedule the next series. The deworming history is important for the same reasons and will also indicate potential problems. Any horse with a questionable or obviously inadequate deworming history should immediately have a fecal examination. Such a horse may require special isolation and deworming treatments before he can safely be integrated into your regular farm routine without contaminating other animals or the premises. He is also more likely to suffer from parasite-related damage to the intestines and their blood supply, leading to chronic colic and digestive difficulties. This is a significant problem at any age but can be seriously debilitating for the older horse.

It is always advisable to get the details of a horse's diet so that changes can be made gradually. Older horses are particularly intolerant of feed changes (grain or hay), and this sensitivity is often compounded by a lifetime exposure to parasite damage. If a horse is receiving any special supplements, ask why. These can often be eliminated or another product substituted with no ill effects. Be alert to any great discrepancy, between a horse's condition and his diet. The thin horse receiving a generous amount of graincould have any number of underlying medical problems, as could the fat or bloated horse on starvation rations. Although this may prove to be only an individual variation in an otherwise normal horse, your veterinarian will be alerted to check for other signs of disease.

You should also commit yourself to an exhaustive effort to uncover a horse's past medical history. This information is immensely useful to the veterinarian performing your prepurchase examination. It will help him or her to focus special attention or testing on previous problem areas and to better evaluate the significance of the current examination findings.

The past medical history will help your veterinarian to diagnose and treat problems the horse may develop in the future should you buy him.

There are three main sources for this information:

1. Recollections of present and past owners
2. Farm health records
3. Veterinary records

The first category is the least likely to be reliable, both for completeness and accuracy, but may contain data not otherwise available. Again, the seller is not going to volunteer this type of information; detailed questioning is needed. Cover all the major organ systems in detail and try to obtain information from the present owner, trainer, and groom, as well as past owners and caretakers.

The following is a list of suggested questions arranged by organ systems.

1. SENSES

A. Vision

Is there any history of shying, "jumpiness," bolting, twisting over jumps, reluctance to move from bright to dark areas or vice versa?

B. Hearing

Is the horse ever startled by your presence when you come into sight from the rear or side? Does he respond when other horses whinny at feeding time or from the pasture?

2. GASTROINTESTINAL

A. Teeth

Does he drop his feed, throw it around, salivate heavily into the feed tub, or pass whole grain in his manure? Does he salivate heavily when a bit is in his mouth? (Simply playing with the bit, or heavy salivation if the horse is a puller, does not necessarily mean there is a problem with the teeth.)

B. Intestines

Has he ever had colic? How often? Is there any history of diarrhea? Does he react badly to worming drugs (often a sign of heavy parasite loads)? Is he a "hard" or "easy" keeper?

3. HEART/LUNGS

Does he sweat or blow unusually hard or long after work? Is he hard to condition? Does he ever cough in the barn? How often does he have respiratory infections? Is there ever a heavy or other than clear nasal discharge? Does he ever breathe hard at rest? Have you ever been told he has a murmur, allergy, or heaves? Have you ever heard, or been told he has, a noise with breathing?

4. MUSCULAR

Has the horse ever "tied up" or had dark urine after exercise? Is there any history of back or flank tenderness?

5. URINARY

Does the horse ever strain to urinate or pass discolored urine? If a gelding, is there any history of excessive behavior of dropping the penis? If a mare, is there an unusual amount of "winking" or squirting urine, even when not in heat?

6. SKELETAL/JOINT

Is there any stiffness in the morning or before work? Is there any marked preference for one lead or one posting diagonal? Is there any history of lameness? Does the horse wear special shoes (and why)? Have there been any leg injuries? Are there any known recent leg problems? Is there a history of foot abscesses or cracks?

7. REPRODUCTIVE (IF NEEDED OR APPROPRIATE)

Stallion: Number of mares bred per season? Breedings per mare?
    Conception rate?
Mare: Number of foals? Date of last foaling? Years barren (bred but no
    conception, early loss of pregnancy)? Years open (not bred)? Any
    known infections or injuries?

Next, ask if the seller has kept written health records and if you may have
a copy.

Finally, identify the veterinarian currently caring for the horse and those
past owners have used, as well as any hospitals or clinics where the horse
was treated. Ask the owners if they will sign a release form so that the
records (or copies) can be turned over to your veterinarian. The release
form itself can be simple: "I authorize the release of all medical records
for the horse _____ to Dr. _____ ."
Legally, the owners can authorize the release of the records to anyone
they choose, including themselves or directly to you; however, such trans-
fers tend to go more smoothly from doctor to doctor.

Such information is extremely valuable, both before and after purchase.
It is unreasonable to expect any older horse to be completely free of problems. The weight you attach to any given difficulty will depend upon the
use you have in mind for the animal and/or the degree of risk you are
willing to assume. For example, a horse in the early stages of chronic
lung disease may have periods during which his breathing is completely
normal, and even an examination of his chest by the veterinarian will be
within normal limits. If you happen to be looking at the horse during
such a period and do not ask detailed questions about his respiratory
fitness, you could easily be buying a hidden problem. Such a horse must
be expected to have some degree of difficulty down the road, with associated treatment costs and loss of use. If you know of the problem before
purchase, you can take the time to become familiar with the implica-
tions of owning such a horse and will be geared for proper and timely
treatment when and if a problem does develop after purchase.

Even the most carefully conducted questioning will leave gaps. However, with the answers you receive, the veterinary records, and the history obtained from past owners, a fairly reliable medical profile can be
constructed.

It is no secret that most people do not go to such lengths to investigate
their potential purchases, and the seller may be surprised by all the questions and special requests. However, there is no reason for the seller to
withhold the above facts or resent your questions as long as he is not
approached in a hostile or suspicious manner. Anyone who absolutely

refuses to comply with your requests for information may be covering up a significant problem.

THE VETERINARY EXAMINATION

Once the horse's medical history data are compiled and you have ridden and examined the horse under a variety of circumstances, it is time to proceed with the veterinary examination. There are two opposing schools of thought regarding the prepurchase examination for an older horse. One holds that you must expect some physical problems and therefore a prepurchase examination should be very rigorous and unbending. The other likewise acknowledges an increased likelihood of problems but claims that scrutiny should therefore be less critical than for a younger animal. There are solid considerations on both sides, and the person who attempts to rigidly follow either is doing a disservice to the veterinary examination.

The guidelines for a prepurchase examination ("soundness exam") are basically the same for a horse of any age. It is vitally important to realize the examination cannot do more than inform you of any deficits present on the day the horse is examined. This is why you must make every effort to obtain the background information on performance, routine health care, and previous medical problems discussed earlier. (Provide the veterinarian with a list of the questions you have asked and their answers at least one day in advance so that any clarifications can be made and tentative decisions can be reached about areas to be X-rayed or given other special evaluation.) However, even with an extensive chronicle and a free hand to perform any indicated tests, your veterinarian still cannot, and should not, guarantee future performance.

This qualification does not mean that the prepurchase examination is unimportant. An aged horse is analogous to a used car. Every effort should be made to avoid investing in an animal that will not reach your expectations and has little ultimate resale value. You may have to accept some battle scars that make him a less-than-perfect physical specimen, but that decision should be based on a thorough and systematic examination.

A complete examination consists of several stages. The horse should be examined at rest, while jogging in hand or on a longe line, and under saddle. When under saddle, he should be observed during and after a work that approximates the activity you will be expecting of him. In some cases, this may require the veterinarian to conduct the examination over more than one day. While such scheduling may be difficult, skipping any part of the exam could yield false results.

The following is a description of the examination your veterinarian will perform and the areas that require special attention. This is not to say you could not check a number of these things yourself. In fact, by taking a close look on your own you may be able to eliminate an unsuitable horse without the expense of the veterinary examination or pick up some things you would like the veterinarian to investigate very carefully.

Every good examination begins with a system. If you always use the same sequence in inspecting the various areas of the horse, the chance of missing something is greatly decreased. A good working system would be the following:

1. Observe the horse from a distance
2. Examine the body from head to tail: head, neck, chest; near side; belly; hindquarters; far side
3. Examine legs and feet: near and far front, near and far hind
4. Observe the horse in motion

There are some practical reasons for following this routine. For example, by beginning with the head and neck, you will have sufficient time to accustom the horse to being examined and also get a feel for his personality and stable manners from a safe vantage point. (Remember, the horse has not been foaled that "never kicks"!) Next, by placing examination of the body before the limbs, you force yourself to pay adequate attention to the whole horse instead of skipping to the part most people find particularly absorbing: the legs. It is also wise to examine the front and hind legs together so that subtle differences from right to left will be more obvious. Be aware that the horse may become a little agitated with the sequence of the leg examination if he is used to having his feet picked in the order of near front, near hind, far hind, far front. Finally, it is logical to proceed to watching the horse move immediately after noting any questionable areas on his legs.

Observation from a Distance

Step one, observation from a distance, should be done when the horse is loose in his stall or turned out, not while he is being held or cross-tied. The purpose is to form an overall first impression and to detect mannerisms such as preferentially resting or pointing one leg, which could indicate soreness. This is also a time to check for symmetry from right to left by observing the horse from as many different angles as possible. As soon as the horse is caught, look him over from front, back, and either side before moving in for the detailed examination.

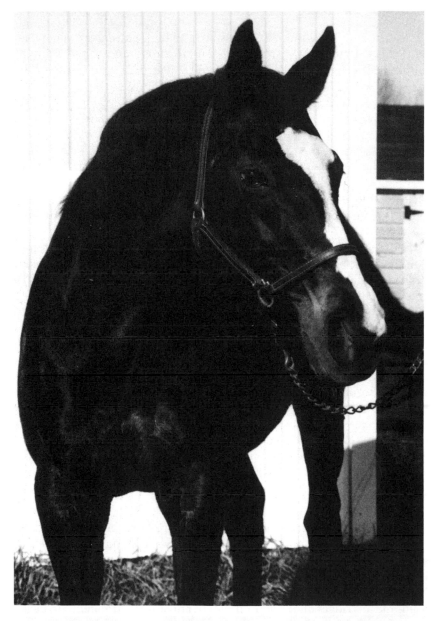

"Night Flight" a 21-year-old Thoroughbred gelding owned by Audrey Petschek of New Canaan, Connecticut, is a good example of how eyes should be widely open and free of discharge and nostrils comfortably wide for good air movement. Photograph by Audrey Petschek.

Ears, Eyes, and Mouth

The examination should begin with the head. Teeth merit special attention in the older horse. It is normal for the upper teeth to overlap the lower ones both in front and on the sides; however, a dramatic overbite of the incisors (called a "parrot mouth") should be avoided. Broken teeth are prone to infection, and missing teeth may affect chewing. The outer edges of the upper back teeth and lingual (toward the tongue) side of the lower arcade should be checked for sharp edges or "points" that form when the teeth are not regularly filed ("floated"). Finally, the last cheek teeth should be examined for large sharp hooks that form when floating is not done properly. (This is an extremely common problem as reaching these teeth is very difficult in most horses.) The mouth in general should be pink, moist, and free of unpleasant odors or breaks in the mucus membrane.

Nasal passages should be wide and free of any white or yellow discharge. You should be able to see the glistening of the mucus membranes inside the nose without moving the upper part of the nostril out of the way. The veterinarian will examine these areas carefully, as well as the sinuses, for normal conformation and signs of tumor or infection.

The horse should hold his eyes widely open, and they should be free of discharge or white color in the cornea (indicating a scar). The pupils should react by becoming smaller in bright light. Although complete examination requires an ophthalmoscope, much useful information can be gained by observing behavioral clues such as reluctance to move from bright to dark areas or shying, which could indicate visual problems.

Hearing can be checked by rattling a feed tub when the horse is not looking or making a sharp noise outside the stall. Also, the base of the ears should be checked for tumors or cysts.

The Respiratory System

A thorough examination of the chest and upper respiratory tract also requires a veterinarian, but a prospective buyer can make many helpful appraisals. The area between the jaws at the top of the neck contains the larynx and throat. It should be wide enough to admit a medium orange. The trachea, or windpipe, lies along the midline of the neck, feels very rigid, and has ridges like a vacuum-cleaner hose—the tracheal cartilages. At the top of the neck it is possible to partially encircle the trachea and apply finger pressure along its sides. If it feels mushy and compresses easily, or if pressure produces a cough, irritation is present. The respiratory rate at rest is normally eight to twelve breaths per minute. The chest should move equally on both sides and respiration should appear effortless. Horses with chronic lung disease may show a double effort and a prominent use of the muscles along and behind the arch of the ribs when they exhale. This is called a "heave line" and indicates trouble moving air (see Chapter 9).

During and after exercise, the horse should be watched for any unusual noises, discharge, or difficulty out of proportion to the work. The veterinarian will also check the lungs at this critical stage and, if indicated, may examine the throat and larynx with an endoscope—a long, flexible tube with a light source that is passed through the nostril.

General Condition of the Horse

The skin, coat, and general condition of a horse are nonspecific indicators of disease and health. With an older horse, pay particular attention to any lumps or growths. This is especially important with gray horses, which commonly develop tumors called melanomas in their later years. Melanomas usually begin in the anal area and along the undersurface of the tail and are thus easily overlooked. Your veterinarian can check for

"Sam," who is 30 years old, is a good example of legs that were built to last, with short sturdy cannon bones and pasterns, as well as a good angle to the pastern. He is owned by Anita Sohus of LaCanada, California. Photograph by Anita Sohus.

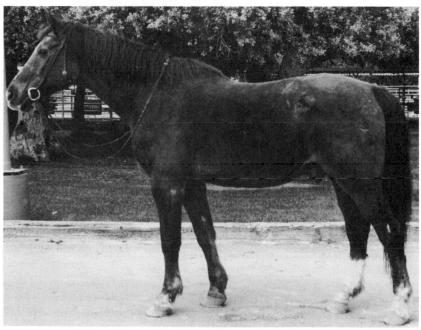

internal spread with a rectal examination. You should also be wary of a horse that does not shed out properly or on time as this may be a sign of a pituitary tumor in the brain, another problem associated with age.

You can tell a great deal about how the gastrointestinal tract is functioning by the horse's general condition, appetite, and amount and quality of manure. In addition to listening to the abdomen with a stethoscope, the veterinarian should perform a rectal examination to evaluate the condition of the intestinal arteries (often severely damaged by a lifetime's exposure to parasites) and to check for other abnormalities such as tumors or abscesses. With the latter, even a rectal exam may fail to detect the problem if the mass lies far to the front of the abdomen or down along the lower abdominal wall. (Note: The seller may rightfully not wish a rectal to be performed as there is always a risk the rectum could be perforated. While the chances of this happening are extremely small, the result can be disastrous. Also, the veterinarian may wish to have special accommodations for restraint in the case of a rectal examination. For these reasons, it is wise to discuss this matter with both parties before the time of the prepurchase examination.)

The Musculoskeletal System

The area of primary concern to everyone is the musculoskeletal system. Always begin by comparing the muscles on either side. Any asymmetry could indicate pain in the leg has resulted in decreased use and concomitant loss of muscle bulk and strength on the affected side. Loss of muscle evenly over the hindquarters may also signal a chronic problem with tying-up or altered blood supply. Palpate the muscles along the spine and croup for signs of spasm and tenderness that usually correlate with a hock or stifle lameness. (Note: This last examination should be done with extreme caution. The horse will often stand quietly while you palpate his back until a single point of tenderness is reached. The speed and ferocity of his reaction to pressure there may take you completely off guard.)

Proceeding to the legs, there should be good muscling above the knee and hock. The lower legs should be as close to a perfectly straight support as possible, and a line perpendicular to the ground should travel directly through the center of the knee, cannon bone, fetlock joint, and point of the toe (see Figure 1a). Deviations result in concussive and compressive forces being concentrated in the deviated area rather than traveling directly through to the foot. This is a defect at any age, but as even minor problems are compounded in time, it is particularly important in all older horse, especially if his trimming has attempted to eliminate any abnormal gait (e.g., paddling) that was a direct result of his anatomy.

Figure 1

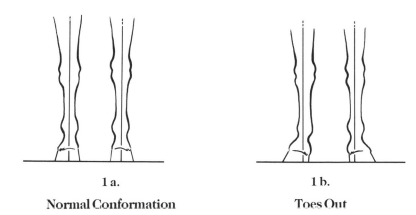

1 a.   1 b.

Normal Conformation   **Toes Out**

If there is crookedness to a leg, particular attention should be paid to those joints where the deviation occurs. A common fault is toes pointing outward from the fetlock down (Figure 1 b). This places strain on the inside of the fetlock joint, which must bear the weight without benefit of support from the pastern and foot. Such horses will paddle (swing the leg to the inside or outside) when they move. This depends usually on whether they are base wide or base narrow (feet positioned inside or outside of a line drawn down from where the legs leave the chest). This often leads to "corrective" shoeing and trimming that eliminates the paddling but makes the strain worse. When the foot is trimmed to bring the breakover point of the toe back under the knee instead of in line with the pastern, a further break in the straight line through the bones to the ground is added at the coffin joint level and ringbone may result, as well as sidebone formation and formation of navicular bone spurs on one side.

If you spot any deviation from normal in the axis of the leg, inspect the involved joints carefully for heat or swelling. Equally significant is a decrease in joint fluid (your veterinarian will check for signs of this). It may be advisable to X-ray such joints before purchasing the horse (more on X-rays follows).

The technique of pinpointing potential problem areas by drawing a line through the leg to the ground is a simple one. Once you master the technique, you will be amazed at how much easier it becomes to zero in on a lameness. For best results, stand the horse squarely on level ground and take a photograph from directly in front and directly behind. You can then examine these at your leisure, using a ruler or straight edge. When able, X-rays are even more helpful in studying the alignment of the bones and the appearance of unilateral bony changes, such as navicular spurs or sidebone. They can also provide clues as to how long and how severely the conformation and/or trimming has been stressing the legs.

The next step is to actually run your hands down every inch of the legs. There are four major things to look for:

1. Heat
2. Swelling
3. Tenderness
4. Asymmetry

Of these, asymmetry is the easiest to detect and the most revealing. Even a relatively inexperienced examiner can notice a difference in two legs. The veterinarian will make a more detailed examination, including the inspection above, and evaluation of range of movement, and flexion tests.

Always pay special attention to the feet. An obvious change in angulation from the pastern bone to the hoof, when viewed from the side, may indicate old founder or fracture. Rings on the hooves indicate founder, change

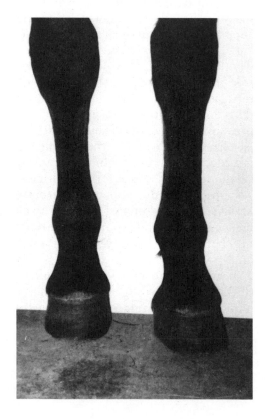

This horse's right cannon bone slants inward, but his right fetlock, pastern, and foot are centered better under the knee. He has been barefoot for quite some time and has worn the feet fairly short, but the breakover point of both toes (visible as a subtly squared-off area) is properly worn in the line with the center of the fetlock joint in both legs. His entire left front leg turns out severely, this straining the inside of the leg. However, his knee, fetlock, and foot are in proper alignment to each other, thus allowing the forces to be transmitted equally to all joints.

in nutritional status, or a severe disease like pneumonia with high fever. The heels are very important. Narrow heels and a shrunken frog correlate with navicular disease or any painful problem in the foot. (An exception would be for Saddlebreds that wear an artificial foot and do not normally have direct pressure on their soles. They may show some atrophy of the frog and/or narrowing at the heels.) Uneven heels reveal the horse is landing harder on the side with the higher heel, either because of pain on the other side of the foot or because of improper trimming. Finally, if the horse is shod with anything other than a plain, flat shoe, get an explanation.

The Horse in Motion

Evaluating a horse in motion requires considerable experience. The veterinarian will be of much help here. Your opinion of how attractively a horse moves may very well be important to the decision of whether or not to buy the horse but does not necessarily relate to his actual soundness. There is one way of detecting even subtle lamenesses and/or gait imbalances that can be mastered by anyone and uses a sense you would not normally rely upon—your hearing.

The better your sense of rhythm and concentration, the easier it will be to learn this. Simply listen to the horse walking and jogging slowly on a hard surface (concrete barn aisles are perfect). If you focus on the cadence of his steps, any interruption to the smooth, almost hypnotically even footfall of a sound, balanced horse will be immediately obvious. Listen first with your eyes closed or back turned and then look and listen together to identify the offending limb. You will probably be more sensitive, at least initially, to a louder footfall. This will be associated with the *good* leg as it takes more weight and lands heavier. Identify the loud leg and look for trouble in the opposite leg. The problem could also be located in the leg that has just given up support. For example, if the right front lands hard, check the left front and left hind.

A sensitive rider can also learn a great deal from the horses back, particularly about the hindquarters. Any reluctance to assume either lead or a marked difference in the feel of a posting trot to either side should be reported to the veterinarian. Most horses (and riders) have a stronger side, which does not necessarily mean they are lame on the other. However, this conformation may back up a subtle impression of trouble the veterinarian had from the ground.

X-Rays

The final stage in a veterinarian's examination is the taking of X-rays. Opinions are as widely separated on this subject as they are on the need of the examination in general. There are those who maintain X-rays are so difficult to interpret they are virtually useless, while others place such stock in them they drift from horse to horse in quest of the perfect set of X-rays.

In many ways, the "nays" have it in this argument, but only because most people's expectations extend well beyond the information any X-rays can provide.

The basic data an X-ray offers is whether an area is normal appearing or not. It cannot tell you if the lesion is currently, or will in the future be, causing pain. There are horses around with fetlocks that are such a mass of extra calcium deposition that the joint is almost unrecognizable, or with sidebone calcification that looks on X-rays like a set of antlers, but the horse is without pain. There are also those with early pathology in the soft tissues, such as navicular or cunean (hock) bursitis, that are terribly lame but appear normal on an X-ray.

A solid approach is to at least take X-rays of the feet. The old saying "No foot, no horse" is all too true. It is also a fact that 60 to 90 percent of all lamenesses can be traced to the foot. You are also more likely to pick up one of the few absolute reasons to turn down a horse, such as early low (involving the joint) ringbone.

The lesson here is not to abandon X-rays, but to use them in conjunction with all the other information from the history and physical examination.

Other Tests

In addition to the physical examination and any X-rays, the veterinarian may suggest any number of blood tests in addition to the normal Coggins. This would be unusual, though, unless some specific problem was suspected. However, it is wise to have the veterinarian store a blood sample for drug analysis in the event the horse goes lame or has a dramatic personality change soon after purchase.

This simple step can protect both buyer and seller from a round of recriminations over who did what to the horse and when. However, such sampling is not routinely done, and the seller may initially take offense at the suggestion. Since there is really no reason to object, tactfully pointing out the benefits while making it clear that such sampling is a condition of sale should settle the question. A seller who refuses to comply must certainly be considered suspect.

As a practical note, it is advisable to inform the seller that you will require blood for possible drug testing well in advance of your veterinarian's arrival. I recall once performing an exhaustive examination with full X-rays from knee and hock down only to have the seller's jaw drop to the floor at the mention of drug testing. They packed up the horse and swept him off in a cloud of protest and indignation, leaving the potential buyer with a sizable bill that probably could have been avoided. Since there is nothing to be gained by surprising people with this testing, give them the chance to refuse before you waste your time and money on an examination.

Making a Decision

At the conclusion of all this testing, the veterinarian will be able to tell you two things. First, if there are any pathological changes in the legs, lungs, and other parts of the horse, and second, if they are causing the horse a problem at the time of the examination, that is, if he is lame, short of breath, and so forth. It is entirely possible for a lesion or disease to be present but not be causing symptoms at the time of the examination, much as you yourself might have an old injury that only aches in certain weather or with certain activities. According to the guidelines of the American Association of Equine Practitioners, the veterinarian should not "pass" or "fail" the horse, and he or she will not be able to tell you if any given abnormal finding will eventually cause a problem. To do either of these things is beyond the scope of a veterinarian's responsibility and requires a crystal ball.

However, while the buyer must make the ultimate decision on purchase, the veterinarian can help by educating him or her on some of the details of the condition(s).

For example, take the common situation where an older horse's X-ray examination reveals changes in the navicular bone. The veterinarian, or a consulting radiology expert, will be able to tell you if the degree of change falls within the "normal" pattern for a horse of that age. This opinion may be further modified if you know the horse's history involved excessive stress (e.g., racing). The X-rays may also indicate if the process is old and slow versus new and active. Add whether or not the horse was moving soundly or had contracted narrow heels or special shoeing, and the possible significance of the X-ray changes becomes more clear.

The veterinarian can also tell you how the activity level you desire of the horse influences the course of navicular disease in general. You then, with the full benefit of the veterinarian's knowledge, must reach the ultimate decision yourself.

2

Routine
Health Care

The basics of a routine health-care program are the same for horses of all ages. Ignoring them is asking for trouble with any horse, but the consequences are likely to be more severe with the aged horse. In many ways, the problems of caring for an aged horse are similar to those encountered with a foal. With specific regard to routine health care, both the aged horse and the foal require rigid vigilance against infectious disease and a wide range of intestinal parasites. They are also less tolerant of improper shoeing and trimming.

VACCINATIONS

One of the consequences of advancing age is a decrease in the ability to fight infections, which become both more likely and more severe. Vaccinations are not a 100 percent guarantee that the horse will not contract an infectious disease, but they do greatly reduce the chances at an investment of time and money that is minuscule compared to the costs of treating a complicated problem. Safe and effective vaccines are available for influenza, rhinopneumonitis, tetanus, and encephalitis.

Influenza

Influenza is the most aggressive viral respiratory infection of horses and can sweep through a group with astonishing speed. This virus commonly causes very high temperature elevations (102° to 104° F), upper and lower respiratory tract disease, and profound weakness. Other manifestations include skeletal muscle and joint pain, effects on the heart (usually limited to electrocardiographic changes), and possible effects on the central nervous system. Perhaps most dangerous is the increased risk of a second, potentially life-threatening or crippling superinfection with bacteria after the virus has compromised the normal defense mechanisms.

Influenza outbreaks generally occur in the colder months when stabling provides for easier spread of the virus, horses are stressed by the demands of inclement weather, and other less serious infections and local irritants (cold air, dust) may all weaken resistance. Initial flu vaccines should be scheduled for the fall, with recommended schedules for boosters ranging from once a year to monthly.

Problems with the vaccine include:

1. Local reaction at the site of injection
2. Mild flulike symptoms
3. Possible triggering of symptoms in horses already infected but not yet ill
4. Failure to provide adequate protection

Reactions at the injection sites are a potential hazard with any vaccine— or any injection for that matter. Manifestations range from slight soreness and/or swelling to the development of massive abscesses resulting in skin loss and requiring surgical drainage and weeks of daily treatment. Sensitivity to the drug itself, or to preservatives, is partly to blame. More significant is the danger of introducing hair, dirt, and/or bacteria with the needle.

The incidence of injection reactions can be greatly decreased by careful cleansing of the skin at injection sites. A quick swipe with alcohol is all but useless; the best technique is a short wash with soap and water, followed by a rinse and a final alcohol and iodine preparation of the skin. If the horse's hair is very long, the area should be clipped or the wash time extended and the hair carefully separated to guarantee the needle only passes through skin. It is no secret that these measures are rarely taken and most horses experience no problems. However, prevention is so simple it is foolhardy to play the odds and inexcusable if there is any history of unusual reaction to vaccines.

A mild flulike syndrome and/or precipitation of disease in horses already incubating the virus is frequently seen with this vaccine. It occurs within twenty-four to seventy-two hours after vaccination and is characterized by decreased appetite, depression, and elevated temperature. The reaction is short-lived unless a full-blown infection evolves. (The vaccine alone cannot cause an infection.) Nevertheless, these immunization reactions, while troublesome, are self-limiting and do not cause any damage to the respiratory tract as will a real infection. It is an acceptable price to pay for subsequent protection.

The final problem, vaccine failure, has two causes. For one thing, the flu virus can and does mutate with relative ease and the strain causing any given outbreak may not be the same as the one used to prepare the vaccine. This new strain can then override the immunization. Also, by preparing a safe vaccine you sacrifice potency. The degree of protection afforded even against the vaccine strain is relatively weak and short-lived so that a particularly heavy exposure to the virus and/or concurrent stressors can lead to vaccine failure. Stressors can include even such nonspecific factors as a cold snap or lameness flare-up.

This problem of inadequate protection has led some veterinarians to experiment with closely spaced serial vaccinations in hopes of maximizing the immune response. This has primarily been tried on racetracks where conditions for spread of disease are excellent. There are no hard and fast statistics on how useful the approach has been, but many feel that vaccinations every four to six weeks result in better control of disease.

The two-year-old and the twenty-year-old horse have remarkably similar difficulties in handling infections. The young horse has an immature immune system while the older one is losing his immunocompetency. The end result is the same—an increased susceptibility to disease resulting in more frequent infections and a decrease in the ability to mount a response to infection, usually leading to more severe clinical signs. Therefore, depending on his exposure level, the aged horse is also a good candidate for the intensive monthly vaccination schedule outlined in the previous paragraph.

To start, the aged horse should be vaccinated against influenza regardless of the anticipated likelihood he will be exposed. The minimum recommended coverage would be a yearly vaccination, given at the beginning of the winter's most severe weather. Based on the veterinarian's experience with vaccine effectiveness, a routine booster in two weeks may also be recommended for all horses.

More frequent boosters, up to as often as once a month, may be indicated in the following circumstances:

1. Frequent movement of horses on and off the farm
2. Population of young horses (under three) also on the farm
3. Horse himself frequently off the farm
4. In the event of an outbreak on the farm or in the vicinity

Vaccination in the face of an outbreak is a controversial topic since the vaccine sometimes seems to trigger symptoms or worsen them in horses already infected. However, it is entirely possible that this apparent triggering really has nothing to do with the vaccine—that is, the horse was going to show signs regardless. The wisest course is to let the veterinarian decide how to proceed, based on his or her experience with the particular outbreak. A common conservative approach is to give boosters only to those horses already vaccinated. The recent vaccine should have provided at least some protection already and will also help the horse to respond much more quickly than an unvaccinated animal, making the booster more likely to be of benefit rapidly enough to help in the face of an outbreak.

Rhinopneumonitis

Vaccination is also available against rhinopneumonitis—literal translation: nose and lung inflammation—which is caused by a herpes virus. Severe rhinopneumonitis infections are limited almost exclusively to young and aged horses, although this same virus can cause abortion in mares.

Several rhinopneumonitis vaccines are available of two general types—modified live intranasal and killed. The modified live preparation is exactly what it says, a preparation of live virus whose virulence has been modified. "Vaccination" in this case is really a controlled planned infection and is done by placing the virus directly into the nasal passages. The resulting disease is usually milder than a natural infection, while the subsequent immunity is stronger than that achieved with a killed vaccine. The killed vaccines are very safe and virtually never cause even mild reactions mimicking infection; however, as with flu vaccine, the immunity is often less than adequate.

Side effects with rhinopneumonitis vaccines include possible local reactions and failure to protect, as discussed in detail for flu. A schedule of vaccination every two months has been reported as satisfactory in controlling the virus. As mentioned, the modified live vaccine can be expected to also cause some illness, usually a slight clear nasal discharge and low-grade fever. It is important not to use the modified live vaccine if the horse has recently had a known exposure to sick animals, been shipped, or been otherwise stressed, as the reaction may be more severe. Finally, modified live vaccines cannot be used to vaccinate broodmares or any animal on a farm where broodmares are kept as it may cause viral abortion.

Tetanus

The tetanus vaccine is the most frequently given equine vaccine—and for good reason. The likelihood of a horse being exposed to tetanus, from the likes of a puncture wound or even a misplaced shoe nail, are high, and an exposed horse can be expected to have severe symptoms and/or die, as horses are very sensitive to tetanus toxin.

Tetanus is a bacteria that is present in the soil and manure. It will not produce toxin unless growth conditions are exactly right—usually in the depths of a puncture wound where oxygen is low. The poison then produces severe spasm of the muscles and eventual respiratory failure.

Tetanus vaccine is available in toxoid and antitoxin forms. The toxoid is a protein that resembles the tetanus toxin chemically and causes the body to produce antibodies that can then inactivate toxin should a real infection occur. This is the regular vaccine that a horse receives as a yearly booster. It takes about two weeks for the antibodies to appear, less on subsequent boosters. Antitoxin is a preparation that can actually bind the tetanus toxin immediately, just as the antibodies of a vaccinated horse would. It is used to provide on-the-spot protection when a horse is at a high risk for infection and/or if his vaccination status is unknown or inadequate. Antitoxin is short-lived, however, and is not truly a vaccine since the body does not respond to it with antibody production. Both of these preparations are often given at the same time when an abscess is discovered—a fairly frequent problem in horses on turnout. The antitoxin is given to provide protection for the seven to fourteen days it takes the horse to produce his own antibodies in response to the toxoid. The only precaution to remember is not to mix these drugs in the same syringe or inject them into the same site, as they may neutralize each other.

Tetanus vaccine, as mentioned, is given yearly and any time the horse is particularly at risk from an injury. There is probably no need to give the vaccine with every injury if the horse is regularly vaccinated, but horses are so sensitive to the toxin that it is best to err on the safe side in such a case.

Encephalitis

Encephalitis is an inflammation of the brain and spinal cord caused by a virus. The disease produces fever, convulsions, and paralysis. There are three strains of encephalitis—Eastern, Western, and Venezuelan. Eastern and Western vaccines are routinely given, and protection against Venezuelan is also recommended in some areas.

Since the disease is carried by biting insects, the usual recommended program is vaccination in the spring in two immunizations, two weeks apart.

Strangles

There are no 100 percent safe and effective strangles vaccines on the market as yet. Part of the problem is that strangles is a bacterial infection and it is much easier to make a vaccine against a virus or a toxin rather than against a bacteria. Several vaccines are available but none are capable of totally protecting the horse if exposed to a large dose of the Streptococcus equi bacterium.

One problem is that the same proteins that the body will identify and make antibodies against in a natural infection cause very severe local and even bodywide reactions when included in a vaccine. This problem has hampered effects to produce safe and effective vaccines for many years. Although those available today are less irritating, reactions are still very common. Manufacturers recommend exercising the horse after vaccination to decrease reactions, presumably by increasing the rate with which the vaccine is absorbed. Other helpful measures include meticulous preparation of the skin to be used as the vaccination site with antibacterial soaps and alcohol, as well as dividing the dose into two sites.

Strangles vaccines, as mentioned above, cannot protect the horse 100 percent. This is certainly true of other vaccines as well but is more of a problem with these. Manufacturers point out, and quite correctly, that a variety of nonspecific factors such as age, stress, nutritional status, severity of exposure, and poor sanitation practices are also involved in whether or not the horse will develop the disease, and how severe it will be.

As a general rule, I do not routinely recommend strangles vaccine for older horses. That is to say, it is not something that I would do on a regularly scheduled basis, as for rabies or tetanus. However, this is a decision that must be made on an individual basis. The horse that is retired and not exposed to new horses on a regular basis is at a low risk for disease. However, an older horse on an active farm, still competing, and/or living in an area or on a farm where there is a strangles problem, should probably be vaccinated.

For those readers unfamiliar with this devastating disease, strangles is so named because a common manifestation is gross enlargement of the lymph nodes located between the lower jaw bones, causing difficulty in breathing. The infection also results in very high fevers and is extremely contagious. This particular bacteria tends to easily form abscesses where the body has difficulty in eliminating the deeply seated infection. The greatest danger with strangles is that it will spread beyond the lymph nodes mentioned and become seated elsewhere in the body. Commonly affected sites include the skin, lungs, kidneys, and abdomen, although once an infection becomes widespread virtually any organ or area may be involved. Young adult horses rarely show a widespread form and may even appear free from clinically evident disease even in the middle of an outbreak. However, foals and older horses are at high risk for very serious infections that could be fatal or cause irreversible damage.

Rabies

Although safe and effective vaccines for rabies have existed for years, it is often a vaccination that is overlooked. Horses are just as susceptible to rabies as any other animal and equally capable of spreading it to other animals or to humans through their saliva. The recent rapid spread of rabies in many areas of the United States makes vaccination a must.

Horses on turnout are at high risk for exposure to wild animals with rabies. However, stabling alone is not a guarantee. The last case of rabies I encountered was in a horse stabled on a racetrack! Close questioning later revealed a groom had noted a racoon near the shed row on several occasions.

Rabies in horses is one of the so-called "dumb" type. Horses do not become agressive and attack in the way that dogs, cats, and wild animals do. Instead, they become markedly depressed, incoordinated and ataxic. Salivation is a prominent sign. Seizures may occur. Paralysis of the penis can be seen as well. Conditions that can be confused with rabies include encephalitis, botulism, lead poisoning, choke, tetanus, or injury/irritation of the mouth.

Vaccination is done at yearly intervals.

Potomac Horse Fever

Potomac horse fever is an intestinal tract disease caused by a rickettsial organism. It is probably transmitted by ticks, with the disease existing in a population of wild animals that serve as a reservoir.

Early signs are fever, depression, and decreased abdominal sounds with depressed appetite. Except for the fever, spasmodic colic might be suspected. Within twenty-four to forty-eight hours, profuse diarrhea begins and may last up to ten days. Laminitis is a frequent complication. Fatality ranges from 17 to 36 percent.

Vaccinations are yearly and should be done in early spring, following the same recommendations as for encephalitis in your area.

DEWORMING

All horses have a lifelong requirement for an effective, rigorously followed deworming regimen. Unfortunately, it is the older horse that is

most likely to be shortchanged in this regard, partially through a mis-
guided impression that the older horse is less troubled by worms. In fact,
his need for good deworming practices actually increases with time over
the age of approximately ten to twelve, and many aged horses lose the
immunities they had in their young adult years and show parasite burdens more like a foal's. Significant loads are acquired more easily, and
the horse may also show susceptibility to more species of worms, such
as roundworms.

Factors to consider in formulating an effective program for any given
horse include exposure, age, and general condition. The horse that is
kept in a boarding stable may very well be exposed to other horses whose
owners are not adequately deworming them. Even temporarily placing
a horse in another animal's stall can result in significant infestation if
that animal was heavily parasitized. Turnout carries its own special set
of requirements that will be discussed in Chapter 15, but it must also be
remembered that exposure is guaranteed if your horse is turned out in
paddocks regularly used by other horses.

Trying to control exposure under conditions such as these is fruitless.
The best you can do is hope to routinely remove any acquired loads. The
traditional approach is to deworm at intervals, using different drugs to
avoid resistance problems (see Table 1). A variation of this approach is
to deworm at intervals but to use only ivermectin, which is active against
all parasites and does not have resistant problems that other agents have.
The newest approach is to prevent infestations entirely by deworming
with daily doses of pyrantel pamoate.

Another approach might be to have routine fecal examinations done to
check the egg counts and then perform additional dewormings as needed.
The problem with this approach is that fecals would have to be done every two months or so, particularly if new horses are frequently added to
the group. Also, a fecal examination is often "closing the barn door after
the horse has left," since it will detect only mature, egg-laying worms,
while it is often the immature, non-egg-laying lifestages that actually do

Table 1

Minimum Effective Deworming Schedule—Rotation Technique

October	Dichlorvos, trichlorfon, ivermectin, or piperazine with carbon disulfide
February	Benzimidazole group
June	Pyrantel pamoate, morantel tartrate, piperazine combinations, or ivermectin

Table 2

Deworming for Potential High Risk*—Rotation Technique

October	Dichlorvos, trichlorfon, ivermectin, or piperazine with carbon disulfide
December	Benzimidazole group
February	Pyrantel pamoate, morantel tartrate, piperazine combinations, or ivermectin
End of May or Early June	Benzimidazole group
August	Pyrantel pamoate, morantel tartrate, piperazine combinations, or ivermectin.

*Piperazine in combination with phenothiazine or ripercol is recommended at least once yearly (March, end of April, or August worming).

Table 3

Deworming for Known High Exposure*—Rotation Technique

October	Dichlorvos, trichlorfon, ivermectin, or piperazine with carbon disulfide
December	Benzimidazole group
March	Pyrantel pamoate, morantel tartrate, piperazine combinations, or ivermectin
End of April	Pyrantel pamoate, morantel tartrate, piperazine combinations, or ivemectin
Mid-June	Benzimidazole group
August	Pyrantel pamoate, morantel tartrate, piperazine combinations, or ivermectin.

*Piperazine in combination with phenothiazine or ripercol is recommended at least once yearly (March, end of April, or August worming).

Table 4

Alternative to Rotational Approach—Especially Appropriate for All Older Horses

Year round	Daily pyrantel pamoate
October	As above

the most harm. Since the cost of a fecal examination is often similar to an actual deworming, this approach could easily wind up being the more expensive, and even less effective, course. If you still plan to use a rotational approach to deworming, the best method is probably to follow Table 3, "Deworming for Known High Exposure—Rotation Technique," and double-check parasitization with a fecal in late June or early July, when the numbers of egg-laying adults in the intestines will probably peak.

The regimen of daily doses of pyrantel pamoate (Strongid C) is the best approach to the problem of parasites. Significant problems can be avoided completely using this method, making it an excellent choice for animals of any age but particularly so for aged horses whose immunity may be poor. You will need to deworm periodically for bots using another agent. Ivermectin is a good choice for this since it has the fewest side effects.

Strongyles

There are many dangerous parasites that inhabit the intestinal tracts of horses. The most damaging of these are probably the large strongyles, or "bloodworms." Strongyle eggs are remarkably resistant to drying or cold temperatures and can lie dormant for months, only to be activated and hatch to the infective larval stage when weather and moisture conditions become ideal. Because the larvae do not travel too far from manure, adults (unlike foals) often gain some protection from their habit of grazing and defecating in separate areas. Some horses (usually stallions or geldings) even keep an organized stall with one corner always used for defection. However, this behavior is only partially effective for horses turned out on large expanses of good grass, and it tends to break down entirely for horses in stalls (unless the stalls are religiously cleaned and picked out several times daily) or on turnout but being fed and hayed in the same area.

Also, nature tends to hit horses hardest when conditions are ideal for the parasite, with evidence suggesting that strongyles actually lay more eggs in the spring than in colder months.

Strongyle eggs hatch outside the horse when the conditions are favorable, and it is these "first stage larvae" that actually infect the horse. The strongyles, in their immature form, enter the wall of the intestine and travel extensively in the blood vessels. Their infections are "invisible" in that fecal examinations may show no eggs. However, heavy numbers and/or repeated exposure over the horse's lifetime result in thickening and narrowing, or even complete blockage, of vital arteries. The result is a recurrent problem with colic or even destruction of a portion of bowel and death of the horse. Parasite-related deaths are not at all unusual in yearlings from contaminated farms. This is also a very real danger for the older animal.

Strongyles have a remarkable capacity to develop resistance to many of the commonly used dewormers (see page 28). It is not enough to use a drug with a different name each time you deworm your horse as many of the preparations are in the same chemical family and the worm will be resistant to the whole group.

Roundworms

Parascaris (roundworms) are also a potential problem for older horses. Again, this is a problem usually associated with foals, and young adults are rarely, if ever, affected. Susceptibility to roundworms returns, however, in a significant number of aged horses, and it is mandatory that drugs with high activity against this parasite be routinely included in the deworming protocol.

Other Intestinal Parasites

Yet another parasite usually harmless in young adult horses is Strongyloides. Foals and aged horses, however, may develop a severe diarrhea with dehydration and electrolyte imbalances when the burdens are large. Strongyloides are found in the small intestine where they attach to the lining. Irritation is generally mild unless large numbers are present. They are sensitive to the thiabendazole group and other common dewormers, and any of the schedules for deworming found in this chapter will cover Strongyloides.

Other parasites found in the large intestine include tapeworms and Oxyuris (pinworms). These are rarely associated with severe problems, but can be troublesome in large numbers, which is precisely the most common result as the older horse begins to lose his immunity to parasites.

Bots and Other Stomach Parasites

The inhabitants of the stomach include Gasterophilus (bots), Trichostrongylus, and Habronema. Of these, bots are the most likely to cause a problem. They are spread by the bot fly, which attaches its yellow sticky eggs to the face and legs of the horse. Eggs on the face hatch spontaneously and the larvae enter the mouth. Eggs on the legs are stimulated to hatch when the horse rubs or licks the area.

The larvae mature in the stomach in about one month and attach to its lining, causing local ulcerations and irritation. They fall off on their own

in eight to ten months time. Large numbers commonly result in digestive upsets and poor appetites, notably for grain.

Dewormers

As mentioned, when using the rotation approach to deworming, a key
consideration in developing a deworming schedule is the question of drug
resistance. This is primarily a problem with the large strongyles (bloodworms). Small strongyles (Strongyloides), roundworms, and pinworms
do not seem to develop resistance. The following discussion will list drugs
by their generic names, not trade names, as different companies may
market the same compound under a different name. It is a good idea to
learn to read the labels to identify exactly what you are giving the horse.

The benzimidazole family includes thiabendazole, mebendazole,
cambendazole, fenbendazole, oxfendazole, and oxibendazole (drugs with
the suffix "azole"). These range in effectiveness from 90 to 100 percent
against large strongyle adults and are 100 percent effective against small
strongyles, roundworms, and pinworms. Resistance is a problem with
this family, and it develops more quickly if the compounds are used
heavily. Rotating the different drugs does not help and can actually increase the rate at which resistance develops. One exception seems to be
oxibendazole, which retains effectiveness in clinical trials even when the
other benzimidazole drugs fail.

Some of the benzimidazole drugs have also been used at two to ten times
the usual dose to treat the immature large strongyles. Side effects may
include decreased appetite, colic, or founder. It is unclear what causes
these effects, but a likely explanation is that the body is reacting to the
death of a large number of parasites. Side effects may be prevented or
minimized by treating the horse with antihistamines and anti-inflammatory drugs such as low-dose steroids before giving the larvicidal dose.
It is not a good idea for an owner to administer a larvicidal dose without
veterinary supervision because of the risk of side effects. You can avoid
the veterinary deworming by using ivermectin yourself. Regular doses
kill larvae. However, if a heavy burden is suspected, pretreatment by the
veterinarian is advisable with this agent also.

Phenothiazine in combination with piperazine is an effective alternative when treating for strongyle infestation. It also works well against
the small strongyles, pinworms, and roundworms. Piperazine with
ripercol is another available combination for the same parasites. The
only drawback is that these drugs usually require administration by stomach tube—but they will eliminate any resistance problems from overuse
of the benzimidazole family.

Other alternate drugs for removing the above parasites without encountering resistance problems include pyrantel pamoate, morantel tartrate, and dichlorvos.

Bots are resistant to many of the dewormers above; however, they can be removed with a combination of piperazine and carbon disulfide or with dichlorvos or trichlorfon. Some of these drugs can be purchased in a feed or tack store. Be sure to have an accurate estimate of the horse's weight from a weight tape or, preferably, an exact weight from a scale, as an overdose of these drugs can cause serious side effects in the gastrointestinal tract or cardiovascular system.

A glimpse at the deworming schedules in Tables 1 through 4 will show the recommended time for administering these drugs is listed as October. This is assuming that the fly season ended in September and the bots have had sufficient time to mature (one month). It is common practice to put off the deworming for bots well into the winter. However, this allows an unnecessarily long time for the bots to damage the stomach; some of the bots acquired early in the season may actually have already completed their life cycles and fallen off by the time the horse gets dewormed for bots! The rule of thumb of waiting until after the first frost to deworm for bots is a useful one. It guarantees there will be no new infection after the horse is treated. However, waiting longer than one month after fly season ends serves no purpose. Furthermore, if infestations appear to be particularly heavy any given year, it may be advisable to add a drug effective against bots to the deworming schedule for mid- to late summer to keep the number of mature worms in the stomach to a minimum.

Ivermectin, as mentioned, is unique in that it will kill all the important species of worms, including bots. It is also effective against the immature stages of Stronglylus vulgaris (the bloodworm), giving it unique activity in this regard as well. There are no recognized problems with resistance making it possible to use ivermectin as your sole dewormer. It does cost slightly more than the other drugs, but its unique characteristics make it worth the price.

Finally, there is the hottest new approach to parasite control, daily use of pyrantel pamoate. Although you will still need to deworm periodically for bots, this is the most efficient way to virtually eliminate all parasite problems. I would recommend it strongly for use in older horses.

Deworming Schedules

Armed with this basic knowledge about the pharmacology of deworming drugs, you can next consider the exposure, age, and general condition factors and formulate an appropriate deworming schedule. "Backyard" horses that are expected to have minimal or no exposure to other

horses with questionable deworming histories may be dewormed according to Table 1, "Minimum Effective Deworming Schedule," if they are in
otherwise good condition and not subject to severe stresses of weather,
heavy exercise, or long-distance traveling. If the horse is over fifteen,
however, it is probably a good idea to have the veterinarian perform a
fecal examination to evaluate parasite levels once or twice a year or anytime there is a problem such as weight loss, poor hair coat, colic, or change
in manure. It is important to remember that it is virtually impossible to
completely eliminate parasites from a horse's life. Even if he never sees
another horse, he will continually be a source of reinfection for himself
via contamination of his environment.

If you own more than one horse but still keep them on your own premises, it may still be possible to deworm according to the minimum effective schedule explained earlier. However, horses vary in their ability
to fight off parasite burdens, and you may have one that can contami-
nate the environment the same as ten "normal" horses. This is one instance when it will pay off to use fecal examinations. After initiating your
deworming schedule, you should run fecals at six-week intervals for three
examinations. The reason for the repeated examinations is that the horse
may have two or more different species of worms in his intestine but only
one actively laying eggs. Dewormers are often only very effective against
the active worms, and the dormant species survives. Since any parasites missed by the first treatment will usually become active themselves
as soon as their competition is gone, fecals can uncover a previously undetected burden. If the program is adequate, however, fecals will eventually become negative and stay that way.

If you board your horse at a public stable, you must assume that he is
being highly exposed to parasites on a constant basis. This problem is
controlled when farm management insists that all animals be placed on
the same schedule; however, this does not eliminate contamination from
horses who rapidly develop heavy burdens between worming and/or are
carrying large numbers of immature forms that mature continuously between wormings. Problems also arise from new additions who have not
yet been "cleaned out" on the regular schedule. Table 2, "Deworming
for Potential High Risk—Rotation Technique," or Table 4, can be followed when the population of horses is high but all are regularly dewormed on the same schedule. However, if worming of the other horses is
not controlled by management, Table 3, "Deworming for Known High
Exposure," or Table 4, should be followed for any aged horse. Also, if
your horse is over fifteen and/or is suffering from any chronic problem
that causes him stress (even a lameness), he should probably be placed
on the known-high-exposure schedule even when conditions are controlled as well as possible.

All of this may seem to some to be overkill for what is commonly considered to be a rather routine matter. However, the dynamics of parasite infection are very complicated, and worms have devised a wide rang of mechanisms to ensure their survival. The older horse is at high risk for infection in the best of circumstances and a prime candidate for very large burdens. Add to this the decline in efficiency of his digestive tract as time goes on and the stage is set for problems with weight loss, poor hair coat, decreased stamina, increased susceptibility to infection, and colic. Failure to follow adequate preventative care in this age group is very likely to have troublesome consequences that are not only more expensive to remedy but may be irreversible.

TRIMMING AND SHOEING

Last but not least is the consideration of trimming and shoeing the older horse. The goal here is to relieve (or at least not aggravate) the inevitable arthritic changes of age and to avoid any stress on the legs that might hasten the development of further problems.

The subject of specific corrective shoeing methods will be discussed in the chapter on lamenesses. Suffice it to say here that exotic corrective shoeing has no place in the care of the older horse. Such overzealous "corrections" often create more problems than they solve. At the heart of any shoeing or trimming must be the establishment of a balanced, properly angled foot.

To evaluate if a foot is properly balanced and angled, it is necessary to view it from the front, back, and sides with the horse standing on level ground and also while he walks. From the front, it is important to note if there is any deviation from a straight leg, how the bones of the lower leg are aligned, and whether or not the horse is landing squarely. Figure 2a illustrates an ideal leg seen from the front. In this case, the line drawn from the center of the horse's knee to the ground runs exactly through the middle of the cannon bone, fetlock, pastern, and foot and cuts the foot in half. Such a horse would travel completely straight when balanced.

Figure 2b illustrates a horse that toes out, a common deviation. Such a horse might swing the leg in toward the center before placing it on the ground. However, if the foot is balanced, he will put it down squarely, not land on either wall. Swinging the leg toward the midline is not in and of itself a problem that needs to be corrected. It is a direct result of the horse's anatomy and any attempts to force the leg to travel in a straight line would only put additional strain on an already stressed limb. It can be seen that the weight line (from the center of the knee to the ground) is concentrated more toward the inside of the lower leg. This horse is more

Figure 2

Arrows Show Angulation of Bones in Lower Limb

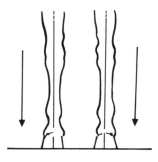

2 a.

Normal Conformation

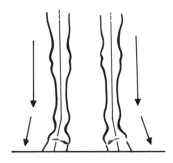

2 b.

Toes Out

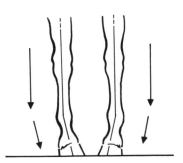

2 c.

Toes In

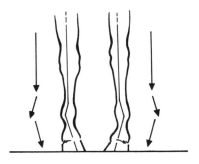

2 d.

Toes Out Conformation with Improper Corrective Trimming

likely to have lameness problems in his medial (inside) splint, suspensory, sesamoid, or medial side of the cannon bone, or to suffer joint-capsule tears on this side. However, unless the axis of the pastern and foot is altered by trimming and/or shoeing, at least the forces can travel in a straight line after being redirected at the fetlock, as shown by the arrows.

The leg in Figure 2c toes in. In this case, weight is concentrated more on the lateral (outside) structures. This horse would be most likely to paddle the leg to the outside before landing. Again, the paddling per se, while not appealing, should not be corrected unless the foot is showing signs of uneven wear from landing to one side.

Figure 2d shows what happens if attempts are made to eliminate paddling or winging in by forcing the foot back under the knee. The line to the ground from the center of the knee has now been shifted so that the breakover point of the toe is aligned with the knee. However, since how the intervening bones are connected cannot really be changed, all that has been done is to add yet another change in direction for the forces traveling down through the bones and joints, as indicated by the arrows. In this case, an added strain has been placed along the outside of the fetlock, pastern, and coffin joints by artificially shifting the hoof and coffin bone out of alignment. This can cause tearing of the supporting ligaments and joint capsules along the lateral surface of the lower leg and may even cause the edges of the bones to be forced together along the medial surfaces. In addition, little to nothing has been done to relieve the initial problem of uneven weight distribution. The result is a horse that now travels straightly but at a tremendous price in strain that can easily cripple an older horse.

When examining from behind, you should focus your attention on the

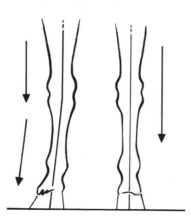

This horse's lower leg is deviated to the outside from the knee down. It should also be noted that the shoe has been properly placed with the center if the toe in line with the cente of the fetlock; however, he has obviously been landing abnormally prior to this as there is a flare to the outside half of the foot and the coronary band on the inside is higher than on the outside.

This leg has the same problem as the leg shown on page 36, but the outside flare has been removed. The coronary band on the inside is still higher, but this will level out in time once the foot has been trimmed to land flat. (The raised coronary band results from landing on that side of the foot.)

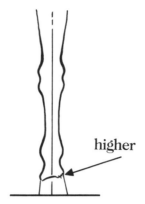

higher

heels (when the horse is standing level) and on whether or not the foot is landing squarely (when the horse is moving). Depending on exactly how the foot is put down, it can be much easier to see an uneven landing from behind. When the horse is standing level, the bulbs of the heels should be of equal height and parallel to the ground. If one side is higher than the other this is referred to as "sheared heels." The higher heel will be found on the side the horse is landing on first as the force of his weight contacting the ground forces up the heel. This is a sign to lower the hoof wall on the side with the high heel. Also significant is a finding of very narrow, contracted heels. This indicates either that the hoof wall is too long and preventing normal contact of the frog with the ground or that the horse is experiencing pain in the back of the hoof (e.g., navicular disease) and avoiding placing full weight on this area. Figures 3 and 4 illustrate contracted and sheared heels respectively.

Finally, view the leg from the side. Figure 5a, illustrates a hoof trimmed to the normal anatomical angle. This results in a straight line from the middle of the fetlock to the middle of the foot. In Figure 5b, the line is broken as a result of leaving too much toe and/or taking off too much at the heels. This is commonly done to increase the horse's stride and cause him to travel low to the ground and with very little knee action (a "daisy cutter"). It is often found in Thoroughbreds that have raced and in show horses. Trimming in this manner puts great additional stress on the tendons and navicular area by causing them to be overly stretched. The fetlock can also be affected, as this joint will drop down farther than it would if the support of the heels were under the ankle where it belongs. The foot in Figure 5c, in contrast, has had too much toe taken off and/or too much heel left on. The result is a shortened stride with high knee action. This increases concussion and jarring and can result in ringbone, sidebone, and any number of other ailments as increased concussion

from improper angulation of the foot aggravates any problems created
by the leg being less that) perfectly straight. The only time it is advisable
to trim a horse in this way is if he is experiencing navicular pain as the
more upright foot does relieve much of the stress in this area.

Occasionally a horse will develop such a tangle of problems related to
angulation of the foot, uneven wear, and lameness that it is difficult to
know how best to trim him. In this case, the best way to proceed is to
balance the foot according to the guidelines presented and then turn the
horse out for a week or so without shoes. If he finds it more comfortable
to carry more heel than "normal" or to land slightly off center, the wear
of the foot will reflect this. It is always best to trim an aged horse according to how he would naturally wear his feet as he knows best how to travel
to minimize any pain that may be present. For more discussion on trim-

Figure 3

3 a.	3 b.
Normal Foot	**Contracted Heels**

Figure 4

Foot Viewed from Behind

Sheered Heels

Figure 5

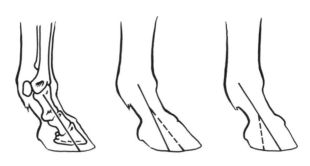

5 a.	5 b.	5 c.
Normal Foot	**Toe Too Long/ Heels Too Short**	**Toe Too Short/ Heels Too Long**

→ = Forces Traveling Through the Bone
- - - - = Break in Normal Allignment of Bones Secondary to Improper Trimming

ming and shoeing, see the chapters on arthritis, turnout, and common lamenesses of the older horse.

Proper attention to routine health-care considerations is more than just a good idea with the aged horse. There is a much smaller margin for error with the older horse as time has decreased his resistance to disease and probably left him with a collection of problems and injuries that will not bear much more insult. It may cost a little more money to care for the older horse properly (it definitely costs more in time and planning), but any problems he develops are more likely to be major and expensive ones. More importantly, it would be a shame to lose a horse that has made it to his later years because of something that could easily have been prevented.

3

Feeding the Older Horse

Nutrition is certainly one of the most basic and important considerations in the care of any animal. However, it is important to note from the outset that there are many gaps in our knowledge about the horse's requirements, particularly regarding vitamins and minerals. This ignorance is probably manifested in the many troublesome conditions and habits that often defy corrective measures, such as wood chewing, poor hoof quality, poor hair coat, pica (a taste for inappropriate items such as bedding, tree bark, and dirt), weight problems, and intestinal disturbances.

The information that is available can be found condensed in the recommendations of the National Research Council (NRC), a publication of the federal government. Their guidelines are a composite of the available research and give minimum recommendations for amount and type of feed in various age and activity categories. Limited research specifically on older horses suggests increased requirements for protein, phosphorus, and vitamin C.

Most brand-name, commercially available feeds are formulated to meet these recommendations when fed with a good mixed hay. Depending upon the management conditions, these may often be the wisest feed choice (although usually slightly more expensive), as their quality and analysis is relatively constant. There are, however, many options in feed formulation and these will be covered in detail shortly.

Before choosing a type of feeding program, you must understand the basic elements of feed and what factors affect a horse's nutritional needs. An appreciation of the complexity of the digestive tract is also helpful. This is discussed in detail in Chapter 7.

The fundamental purpose of feed is to supply energy—calories. Each of the three main food types—carbohydrates, proteins, and fats—supply energy, with fat being the most concentrated source. This energy is used to perform daily activities; to repair and replace body cells; to manufacture hormones, some vitamins, and many other products of the body; and even to aid in the formation of waste products such as urine and manure.

The natural equine diet is extremely high in carbohydrates with smaller amounts of proteins and fat coming from grain and young grasses or early cuttings of hay. The horse's digestive tract is very well designed to make the most of virtually any source of carbohydrate and actually functions best when the carbohydrate is in a very complex form that would be undigestible to species with simpler digestive systems, such as man and the carnivores. In fact, overindulgence in easily digested carbohydrates, such as grain, can lead to severe colic, metabolic disturbances, and founder.

Protein is essential to maintaining the muscles and repairing cells. The horse's minimum daily requirement is not very precisely known, but a level of around 8 percent seems to be tolerated as a lower limit with no grossly obvious ill effects. Diets as high in protein as 18 to 20 percent have been fed to horses—usually to promote growth of young stock. Contrary to some opinions, a high-protein diet (meaning over 12 percent) has not been proven to cause any problems with diarrhea or skin eruptions in older horses. However, it is the most expensive way to provide calories. The horse's sources of protein include grains (oats and barley are high, corn the lowest) and young grasses or early cuttings of hay, most notably the legume hays such as alfalfa.

The horse has a minimum requirement for fats that is very low. However, fats are vital to the maintenance of good hair and hoof quality and to the proper functioning of the liver and other glands. Fats are primarily derived from grains.

In addition to his caloric requirements, the horse must have a high concentration of fiber (undigestible plant material) in his diet in order for his intestines to function properly. His gastrointestinal tract is designed to host a very large and varied population of microorganisms in the large intestine (the cecum and colon). This is an evolutionary development that helps the horse (and other grazing animals) to survive under conditions where vegetation is very sparse and tough. When placed under the microscope, a drop of fluid from the horse's huge colonic system reveals tremendous numbers of many different types of organisms. It looks much like a drop of pond water. These life forms break down the tougher plant materials into simpler chemicals that the body can absorb and use, and they also provide some materials that other organisms of the intestinal tract can use as their food source.

For all its complexity, the system within the colon is actually in a very precise balance. Any change in feed will alter the chemical environment, cause shifts in the various populations of organisms, and possibly result in eventual colic. In addition, if anything happens to drastically upset the balance of organisms (e.g., bad feed, drastically decreased feed intake, internal problem with the blood, or nerve supply to the intestines), the result may be a syndrome of chronic colic and/or diarrhea that is very difficult to reverse.

The older horse has unique requirements for calories, protein, and fiber. On the one hand, his metabolism is slowed so that the baseline need for calories is lower than in earlier years. However, as time goes on, the digestive tract becomes less effective in handling changes in feed, however minor, and this in turn results in an overall decrease in the ability to effectively digest the tougher plant materials. Other factors, such as poor teeth, also decrease his digestive efficiency. Research in other monogastric (one stomach) species shows aging changes include decrease in stomach acid and enzymes, reduced absorption of all nutrients, and decreased motility of the intestinal tract.

With specific reference to the horse, we know that the requirements for protein and phosphorus are increased and that the digestion of fiber is less efficient than in younger animals. Since additional phosphorus must be balanced with a proportionate increase in calcium, these minerals should be supplemented so that the horse receives 40 grams of calcium and 29 grams of phosphorus per day. This is twice the amount required by late yearlings so you will have difficulty doing this by using any available feed. However, feed manufacturers who do a dairy business will be able to supply you with these special proportions in a mineral mix.

It is also recommended that older horses be fed a 10 percent protein diet, rather than the 7 to 8 percent usually called for in mature horses that are not in work. However, these figures are the lower limits and unless you have a very high quality protein source (soybean products, top class alfalfa, etc.), it would probably be wise to use a 10 to 12 percent figure as your guideline.

Decreased digestion of fiber results from a combination of factors which add up to a less varied and efficient population of organisms in the colon. In everyday considerations, this translates into a requirement for healthy pastures or high-quality, early-cutting mixed or legume hay as the staple of the older horses diet. The "average" 1,000 pound older horse that is not in work will need 1.5 to 2.0 percent of body weight of hay per day.

This would be 15 to 20 pounds of hay per day. You can avoid weighing hay every day by taking the time to count the bales in each hay shipment and divide this into the total weight delivered to give you an average weight per bale for each load of hay. However, if even a high-quality all-grass hay is substituted for the suggested hay, protein supplementation is necessary.

Yeast cultures have also been shown to increase the digestion of fiber in the colon. Addition of yeast cultures can improve digestion. Use of a concentrate whose base is brewer's byproducts is also very helpful in feeding the older horse. In addition, there are a number of feed additives on the market that contain live cultures of micro-organisms that normally inhibit the colon. Feeding these may be helpful in some horses.

These minimum recommendations for the "average" horse can only be used as a basic guideline. Anything that causes the horse stress will immediately alter his feed requirements. Such stressors are numerous,

There are several different ways to present concentrates to your horse, such as the textured sweet mix, pellets, and extruded feed shown here.

and many must be considered almost inevitable facts of life. They include work, extremes of weather, lameness, parasite infestation, infections, chronic diseases such as heaves, shipping, change in environment, and reproductive activity. With any of the above, the need for calories increases (with or without an increased need for protein), which basically means that the horse will need a more concentrated feed source in addition to his mixed or legume hay—i.e., grain.

ENERGY SOURCES

The higher feed requirement is basically a need for more calories (in proper balance of vitamins and minerals, which a proper feed will naturally contain). Although it is immaterial whether these calories come from a carbohydrate, fat, or protein source, carbohydrates are the natural and safest choice when trying to boost energy intake. However, if the diet is already borderline in protein, as when only mixed, late-cutting hay and/or only corn as a grain are being fed, it is best to boost the protein content to around 10 to 12 percent to provide at least a small margin of safety. This is particularly important if the stress involves fever or a serious insult to the body (such as a wound or fracture) as protein levels must be raised to help the horse repair tissue breakdown.

Light Use/Stress

Specifically, when stress is minimal—such as light work, a switch from stall maintenance to turnout, or a low-grade but persistent debilitating condition such as controlled heaves or minor lameness the horse should be fed 1.0 to 2.0 percent of body weight of high-quality mixed hay (one-third to one-half alfalfa) and 0.5 to 1.0 percent of body weight of grain per day. This would be approximately one flake per 100 pounds of body weight; but again, it is best to obtain an average weight per bale for each hay shipment you receive as feeding "by the flake" is not accurate. The grain ration may be straight oats, a 70:30 mixture of oats and corn, or a 70:30 mixture of oats and barley. Mixtures should be made by weight of the grain, *never* by volume measures (such as a can of this and a can of that); a can of corn can easily weigh twice as much as a can of oats. The more legume (alfalfa) is fed, the higher the protein content will be. Barley also raises the protein content of the feed, and oats are a moderately good source, being around 10 to 12 percent protein. All of these feeds must be of good quality, with a minimal amount of stem in the hay and full, plump kernels of grain.

An alternative to the above traditional combinations would be 100 percent alfalfa hay and corn as the only grain. This is often less expensive in localities where alfalfa is plentiful. It is ideal for the older horse as the energy content is actually higher than when grass hay and oats are fed, the calcium to phosphorus ratio is in a better balance than when feeding mixed or grass hays, and the protein and energy are of excellent quality and easy to digest.

The very suggestion of feeding straight alfalfa hay and corn may horrify some horsepeople who believe that alfalfa is "too rich" and corn will make the horse "too hot." However, these are myths with absolutely no basis in fact. Straight alfalfa hay will not cause any digestive upsets if the transition from a mixed or grass hay is made gradually, over a period of seven to ten days. There is absolutely no reason why it should be associated with diarrhea either, although the manure may be similar in quality (more soft and more green) to that of a horse on fresh pastures. As for corn, it will not make the horse "hot" in body temperature or "hot" in temperament. The only thing it will do is supply him with a safe, readily available source of energy that will brighten his outlook if his diet had been borderline prior to giving him corn—certainly a desirable effect. The common prejudice against alfalfa hay and corn stems from improper feeding techniques rather than from any problem with the feeds themselves. It is imperative with this or any other change in feed to make the transition gradually, substituting at a rate of approximately 10 percent per day, and always to substitute by weight, not by volume of feed or flakes of hay, as the more energy-rich feeds also tend to be heavier.

Many people prefer to feed a sweet mix rather than the pure grains described above. This is not harmful in any way and molasses is an excellent source of the copper and iron necessary for proper formation of the blood. However, you must be extremely careful about the quality of the feed. Some mills will use their low-grade grains when preparing a sweet feed, and the horse may be getting little more than hulls, dust, and sweetener. Do not use a sweet mix unless it is from a brand-name manufacturer or comes with a guaranteed protein content (which translates into a higher quality of grain).

Pelleted feeds are also popular with some people and are an excellent choice for the older horse. They usually contain grain and alfalfa meal, giving a very good level of easily digested protein and calories (breakdowns are available from the manufacturer). Pellets usually come in several different protein categories. (There are too many different types of pelleted feeds to go into them in detail here.) They are particularly good for the older horse because the grains are highly processed and therefore easy to digest. Pellets tend to be more expensive, but the cost may be offset since with them you can use a lower grade of hay. Some pellets are designed to offer complete nutrition; however, most horses will also need some type of hay to obtain the fiber necessary for proper functioning of the digestive tract and to alleviate boredom. Before switching to a pelleted feed, ask the feed mill representative or your veterinarian how to calculate the amount of pellets and hay to feed to approximate the more traditional diets appropriate for your horse's condition and use.

The newest addition to processed concentrates is the extruded feeds. These are generally held to be the most easily digestible. These may be worth considering for "difficult keepers".

Finally, another exciting "complete feed" option is now available— Horsehage™. Basically, long grass or lucerne is cut, compressed and sealed into plastic bags within 24 hours of cutting. An anaerobic fermentation then takes place that favors growth of yeast and lactate producing organisms.

The result is a product that is highly digestible and very palatable. Horsehage is only 50 percent dry matter (compared to 80 percent for hays), which mechanically helps digestion. Horsehage retains 95 percent of feed value of the original grass, compared to 40 to 60 percent for good quality hay.

It is very high in fatty acids, sugars, and amino acids—all of which can be absorbed quickly and easily in the stomach and small intestine. It is so well utilized that substitution of Horsehage for hay allows grain to be halved or even eliminated. Furthermore, the amino acid content is perfectly balanced.

Horsehage has more calcium than other rations and the yeast fermentation makes it an excellent source of B vitamins.

Finally, the product is dust and mold free, making it ideal for horses with respiratory problems.

Medium Use/Stress

When a horse is in medium or heavy use, or is being severely stressed by illness, lameness, weather, or pregnancy (more will follow about pregnancy), he should be fed anywhere from 1.0 to 2.0 percent of body weight of mixed hay per day and from 0.75 to 1.5 percent of body weight of grain per day. These figures apply to the grain and hay mixtures described for light stress. Again, straight alfalfa and straight corn may be substituted and can be the feed of choice as they are highly palatable, readily accepted, and able to be fed at the lower recommended amounts while still achieving the same energy and protein levels as when offering larger amounts of less dense feeds. This is often an important consideration when appetite is less than good, which is another common result of aging. Pelleted feeds, also very concentrated sources of energy and protein, are likewise worth considering.

During and after any disease with fever and/or bacterial infection, the requirements for protein will be maximal. To boost the protein content and/or the quality of the protein being offered, several different measures may be taken:

1. Gradually increase the percentage of legume hay fed, i.e., substitute alfalfa for grass hay or mixed hay at a rate of 0.5 to 1.0 pounds per day.
2. Eliminate corn in corn and oats mixtures and substitute oats or barley, yielding 100 percent oats or up to 30 to 40 percent barley with the balance oats, at a rate of 0.5 to 1.0 pounds per day.
3. Substitute soybean meal for other grain up to about 20 percent of the grain ration, at a rate of 0.5 to 1.0 pounds per day.
4. Substitute wheat bran for other grain up to about 20 percent of the grain ration, at a rate of 0.5 to 1.0 pounds per day (must adjust for increased phosphorus).

There are many, many other high-protein feeds and feed supplements that can be fed, but these are among the best tolerated by horses and also contain a proper balance of the different amino acids (the building blocks of protein). For example, linseed meal and/or oil is an excellent protein source and also benefits the coat. It is well tolerated by horses, but it is lacking in the essential amino acid lysine. There are many very good protein sources marketed primarily for cattle, but these may put too great a strain on the older horse's digestive system. However, if the horse is already accustomed to receiving such a supplement (a commonly used one is Calf Manna), you can probably increase it to about double the amount he usually gets over approximately one week's time. Another way to boost protein is simply to switch over to a commercial grain mixture with a high protein percentage guaranteed by the manufacturer. Since the protein is usually in the form of alfalfa or soybean it is easily digested. Follow the substitution rate of 0.5 to 1.0 pounds per day when making such a transition.

The recommendations for amount and type of feed under various circumstances will usually be adequate to cover any situation the horse might meet. However, it is of course necessary that the horse actually consume the feed, digest it, and absorb it properly for it to do any good.

To be palatable, a feed must always be clean. Dusty, moldy, or damp feeds are not only distasteful, they may actually be harmful if they contain any mold growth. If your horse has a poor appetite despite high-quality feed, you can encourage eating by feeding several small meals and leaving him without anything to nibble on (including edible bedding) between meals. Stimulating the horse with a short walk or grooming prior to feeding may also help to perk him up a little (remember, the horse that needs his feed the most will often be the ill or debilitated one least likely to have an appetite).

You will find that a horse will often go off his grain before he refuses hay. This is not a problem for a day or so, but he will rapidly become energy- and protein-deficient should this continue, especially if he is severely stressed. This can be partially offset by beginning a switch to straight alfalfa hay. The horse might also be more willing to accept a pelleted feed, particularly one with an alfalfa base, and you can try a gradual switch to this instead of his usual grain ration.

Grain consumption can be encouraged by adding molasses or grated carrots or by incorporating the grain into a warm mash. If these measures fail, it may be helpful to try psychology and add an element of competition (unless the horse is too debilitated or is infectious to other animals). A horse with a problem often feels less like eating, which can be compounded by a boring stall confinement that leaves him little else to do than ponder his troubles. Try feeding the horse outside in a small paddock with another horse (it must be a horse he normally associates with). Their combined rations should be divided up into three buckets. You could also try putting a sheep or goat into the stall with the horse at feeding time. The competition and novelty often spark appetite. Once the horse is back eating grain again you can return to more conventional feeding in the stall.

"Skipper," a 19-year-old American Quarter Horse, continues to provide his owner's family with many happy hours hacking cross-country. He is a good example of how proper nutrition contributes to how a horse looks, feels, and performs. Owned by Richard Sears, Sheds, New York. Photograph by Judy Sears.

Heavy Work/Stress/Pregnancy

Even when a horse is well motivated to eat, a problem sometimes arises with providing feed in a sufficiently calorie-dense form so that he will be physically capable of eating enough without causing digestive upsets. For the healthy older horse this is not a problem. In fact, the normal aged horse usually has more of a tendency to gain weight than to lose it. This is due to decreased metabolic rate with decreased caloric needs. However, with severe extremes of weather, severe disease (primarily infections with fever), and pregnancy you will encounter a long-term, very high requirement for adequate feed intake to meet the basic body needs and the demands of the added stress.

In such cases, it is absolutely imperative that feed quality be high and that the more calorically dense feeds, such as corn or barley for grain and early cuttings of high-percentage legume hay or young pastures, be available. Crimping or rolling oats and cracking corn will make them more digestible and therefore yield more energy for the same weight of feed. You may also boost the caloric intake by adding corn oil to the grain ration. A safe amount of corn oil is up to about one cupful daily, starting with two ounces and increasing by one ounce per day. However, corn oil in amounts over two ounces per day may greatly increase the requirements for vitamin E in the diet, and your veterinarian should be consulted regarding supplementation. In some cases it may be necessary to switch to specialized diets containing products such as dried milk solids or brewer's grains, although this must be done very carefully and under the supervision of a veterinarian.

The aged pregnant mare is a special case as pregnancy itself is among *the* most stressful (and lactation probably the most stressful) conditions in terms of caloric requirements. When you add to this any concurrent problem stressors and the common tendency in late pregnancy to go off feed because of abdominal fullness and general discomfort, it becomes very difficult indeed to get many mares to foaling without a great loss in body condition.

With pregnancy, the cardinal rule again is to feed high-quality feeds. Each day the mare will need from 0.75 to 1.5 percent of body weight of grain and an equal amount of hay. Hay should be the same mixed hay as recommended for other older horses, but at least a 50 percent legume mix. Some good grain combinations might be a mixture of 80 percent oats and 20 percent wheat bran; a mixture of 45 percent oats, 45 percent barley, and 10 percent wheat bran; or a mixture of 95 percent oats and 5 percent soybean meal. These combinations, with the hay, will provide adequate protein and a good calcium/phosphorus ratio (see section on vitamins and minerals), and will be adequate in calories if the mare is otherwise in excellent condition. However, if she is chronically lame, as is often the case, it is best to consult with your veterinarian immediately if you notice any drop in her condition when feeding the maximum recommendations described earlier. It may be necessary to reformulate the ration rather than to try to get her to eat more of the suggested diets.

As a final note on pregnancy, owners are usually cautioned to avoid overfeeding a mare for the first two trimesters of pregnancy as an overly fat mare often experiences difficulty in foaling. This is indeed a wise admonition, but it is also important to remember that the mare's feed requirements will start to rise sharply toward the end of pregnancy when the foal is rapidly growing. The added weight of the foal will also aggravate any lameness she may have, thus adding to her stress, while her increasing abdominal fullness can thwart any attempts to push more feed. For this reason, the owner of an aged pregnant mare, particularly one with any other type of chronic problem, should be more tolerant of a slight weight gain in early pregnancy, fully anticipating she will draw on this reserve before the foal is born. When the mare is late in pregnancy, it is easier to slow down the rate of feed increases (should she remain too heavy or continue to gain) than it is to try to reverse a downward trend in her condition with a feed increase. Also, a mare on a declining plane of nutrition will be more likely to have problems with providing adequate, high-quality milk.

VITAMINS AND MINERALS

In addition to the horse's requirements for adequate calories and protein, it is necessary to consider his needs for vitamins and minerals. We know from extensive research in other species that these substances are critical to the normal functioning of the body. However, when it comes to the horse, there are few hard and fast guidelines as to the amounts that are needed. To complicate matters even further, when such information is available it is often in reference to those vitamins and minerals that are toxic when given in too great an amount—and there is usually a very narrow range between what is necessary as a minimum intake and that which will produce poisoning. Examples of these include copper, selenium, iron, vitamin A, vitamin D, and vitamin E. It is nice to know how much of these the horse should get; however, supplementation cannot be recommended across the board since the levels already present in natural feed sources vary so widely with local soil conditions and the handling of feeds and hay during processing and storage. When it comes to the relatively nontoxic but equally critical substances—such as the B vitamins, vitamin C, and zinc—information on required levels and suggestions for supplementation is often entirely unavailable.

Calcium/Phosphorus Ratio

One area that has been well worked out is the necessary calcium/phosphorus ratio for the horse. These two elements are critical to normal bone growth and adult bone maintenance. The amounts of these minerals that are actually present in the circulating blood and therefore available to the bone cells are controlled very carefully by hormones secreted by the parathyroid gland. These hormones have one purpose: to keep the proportion of calcium to phosphorus in the range of 1.5 to 1.0 in the blood. This is the ideal ratio for bone metabolism and protects the other organs, such as heart and kidneys, from the dangerous effects of too much calcium. To keep this safe ratio, the kidney eliminates any excessive amount of calcium or phosphorus. The result is that the ratio remains intact, but often at the expense of there being not enough total calcium and phosphorus in the body. For example, assume a horse is fed a diet that is too rich in phosphorus, such as very poor quality, late-cutting grass hay and a large amount of grain. The body will react by excreting some of the excess phosphorus to try to keep the ratio normal. Since this diet is also very low in total calcium (the horse's best source being alfalfa hay), the horse may even have to steal calcium from stores in the bone to keep the blood levels normal. This results in weakening of the bone, or "brittle bones"—osteoporosis.

A diet heavy on legume hay and corn will come closest to safely supplying the necessary amounts of these minerals. If anything, the greatest variation is most likely to be in calcium content as this very closely follows the percentage and quality of the legume hay.

The horse over fifteen will need about 29 grams of phosphorus and 40 grams of calcium per day (twice that required by younger mature horses). If he is eating a diet of high-quality, 50 percent legume hay and several pounds of grain per day he is probably meeting all but the increased requirement for age. Therefore, you will need to supply him with 14 grams of calcium and 9 grams of phosphorus per day as a supplement, assuming that his natural diet is perfectly balanced already. In fact, natural diets vary greatly in their calcium/phosphorus ratio and in the total amounts of either element. As mentioned, calcium is likely to be the lowest in total amount while phosphorus total amounts could be more than adequate already. Luckily, the horse can tolerate an excess of calcium (if getting enough phosphorus) without too much trouble, so ballpark calculations on how much supplement to give can revolve around the calcium content of the feed (after ensuring phosphorus intake is adequate). The most commonly used supplement is dicalcium phosphate, which should be fed to meet that extra requirement for aging, that is, 9 grams of phosphorus and a minimum of 14 grams of calcium as a supplement.

Vitamin D

Even when calcium and phosphorus are supplied in adequate total amounts and in the proper ratio, utilization will be hampered if the horse is not receiving enough vitamin D. Vitamin D is the "sunshine vitamin." It is produced by the body when the horse is exposed to sunlight. Therefore, it is not necessary to worry about vitamin D unless the horse is being confined to a stall for a prolonged period of time (over a month for example). When sunlight exposure is decreased, there is some vitamin D stored in the body, which the horse can draw from.

Vitamin D should never be given "just to be safe," as it can be very toxic. Dosing the horse with as little as ten times his required amount may produce weakness; weight loss; calcification in the blood vessels, heart, or other soft tissues such as skin; and abnormalities of the bones. If a prolonged stall confinement is necessary, consult your veterinarian first regarding available supplements. Recommended feed levels for horses deprived of sunlight are 227 IU (Internationa Units) per pound of feed.

Vitamin A

Another vitamin the body stores is vitamin A. Vitamin A is manufactured from carotene, a pigment in fresh green grass and high-quality hay. Under most conditions, the horse eats more than enough of these feeds to supply himself with vitamin A and to store enough to last for three to six months. However, carotene deteriorates with storage, and hays that are over a year old and/or brownish or overly sun-bleached will be deficient in vitamin A. The signs of vitamin A deficiency include eye and skin problems and poor growth in young animals, while feeding excessive amounts can cause toxicity with bone fragility, excessive calcium deposition around the bones, and skin abnormalities. Mature horses need from 30 to 60 IU/kilogram of body weight of horse of vitamin A per day. Supplementation is not often needed, although you might wish to discuss the topic with your veterinarian if your pastures and hays are of borderline quality in any given year. Most commercially available vitamin supplements for horses do contain some vitamin A, and this should be taken into consideration before adding any additional supplements to cover a suspected specific vitamin A deficiency.

Salt

To return to the mineral requirements of horses, their greatest need is for sodium and chloride—salt. These two elements are present in the greatest concentration in body tissues and are absolutely essential to every bodily function. The horse will instinctively regulate his salt intake if he is provided with a salt block. Do not be concerned about even seemingly large differences in salt consumption from horse to horse or in the same horse from day to day. With the exception of times of severe gastrointestinal upset or other dangerous metabolic upset (such as heat stroke), there is usually no way to improve upon the horse's own instinctive regulation of his salt intake. Some horses do appear to consume excessive amounts of salt (usually when bored), but this will not be a problem as long as a constant supply of fresh water is available.

On the other hand are horses who seem to almost never touch their salt. However, it is *never* advisable to add salt to the horse's water supply as this eliminates the horse's ability to regulate his fluid and salt intake and can lead to imbalances that cause dehydration. If a salted water supply, or one containing electrolyte powder with other substances as well, is recommended by the veterinarian during periods of intestinal upset or heavy exertion, it should never be the only source of water. Fresh water must be supplied in a separate bucket, with care taken to assure that the water in both buckets is kept fresh. Horses that need the salt or electrolyte mixtures will commonly consume water only from that bucket for periods of up to several days until their system is replenished. However, should this behavior continue, consult your veterinarian to rule out an ongoing problem.

To summarize, adequate salt is essential to the health of the horse. However, he will almost certainly take in exactly what he needs if free access to a salt block (and fresh water) is provided. When water containing salt or electrolytes is recommended by the veterinarian, be certain to also provide fresh water as well.

Potassium

Potassium is another electrolyte familiar to most people. It is important in proper functioning of the heart and skeletal muscles. Deficiencies result in weakness and irregular heart beat, while excesses can often have similar results. Any horse that is receiving 50 percent of his total ration, in pounds, as hay or other forage is receiving enough potassium for most circumstances. However, some illnesses—such as colic, kidney disease, and muscle disease—and work in hot weather may increase the need beyond what he can obtain in this way. Again, the veterinarian should be consulted for specific recommendations as it is at least theoretically possible to overdose the horse with potassium supplements. He or she will probably recommend either an electrolyte mixture as mentioned on page 50 or direct supplementation with potassium chloride alone.

Copper

Copper is essential to a wide variety of functions, including the normal production of elastic connective tissues, maintenance of red blood cells, production of the pigment melanin, and maintenance of intracellular structures. Recently, research has also strongly suggested a key role for copper in the prevention of metabolic bone disease, osteochondrosis dessicans. (Also see page 171.)

Current NRC (National Research Council) recommendations stand at 10 milligrams of copper/kilogram of diet for horses of all ages. However, levels of three times this are suggested for pregnant mares and five times the recommended level for foals to prevent metabolic bone disease. Although the NRC has not yet officially accepted this research, there is enough information available to warrant "playing it safe" and feeding the higher levels. This is particularly true since horses tolerate copper well and the suggested levels for mares and foals are well below toxic, which stands somewhere around 800 milligrams/kilogram of diet.

Iron

The horse needs iron, as most people know, to maintain appropriate hemoglobin concentrations in the red blood cells. The horse is very efficient at processing and saving the iron present in his body. Since the daily requirement for adult horses is estimated to be 40 milligrams/kilogram (mg/kg) of diet (50 mg/kg of diet for pregnant or lactating mares) and forage and by-products contain 100 to 250 mg/kg of iron, a dietary deficiency is highly unlikely.

Despite this fact, iron remains a widely used/abused supplement, particularly for performance and race horses. High dietary iron can depress both serum and liver zinc, interfering with this essential mineral. Supplementing iron may also adversely effect liver and bone marrow function. Foals fed excessive zinc may actually die, with pathological examination demonstrating erosion of the lining of the intestines, pulmonary hemorrhage, massive iron deposition in the liver and liver degeneration.

Unless the horse has suffered a major blood loss, there is no reason to feed an iron supplement. While the decreased digestive efficiency of the older horse would probably make him more resistant to excess dietary iron, the risks simply outweigh any possible benefits. If your older horse is diagnosed to have an anemia, a complete work up to identify the cause should be carried out before simply feeding an iron supplement.

Zinc

Zinc is a very important element, even though the amounts found in the body and required in the feed are usually very low. It is essential to the maintenance of the eyes, normal coat, and skin, and helps protect against infections. If there is any one element that has failed to receive the research needed to define its functions and pinpoint requirements, it is zinc. Older animals of other species are often plagued by problems related to inadequate amounts of zinc in the diet. A problem with zinc is that high calcium intake may block its absorption. This may be a particularly significant consideration in older horses on high quantities of legume hay and calcium supplements, as discussed on pages 48-49.

As with copper, recent research also indicates zinc may play an important role in the prevention of metabolic bone disease. While the NRC currently accepts a recommendation of 50 mg/kg of diet, these researchers suggest a level of 90 mg/kg of diet be maintained to minimize the incidence of metabolic bone disease. Since mares and foals have been fed levels as high as 700 mg/kg of diet without adverse affect, the higher recommendation is well within safety limits as known by currently available studies.

Too low an intake of zinc may be associated with poor coat, skin, and hoof quality, and increased infections. It is prudent to supplement the aged horse with zinc, and vitamin preparations are marketed that contain this element.

Selenium

There are many other elements that are found in trace amounts in the body, and all perform a vital function. Of particular note is selenium. Selenium is necessary for the proper functioning of skeletal and cardiac muscles and for clearing toxins from the body. Most of the coastal regions of the United States are known to have very low selenium levels in the soil and feeds. The usual manifestation of deficiency is "tying-up," a condition of spasm and muscular breakdown after exercise. The horse is reluctant to walk and obviously in pain, with tense, swollen muscles. He may have red to brown urine that contains muscle cell pigment—myoglobin. Death can even result from damage to the kidneys secondary to myoglobin, or from heart dysfunction and alterations in the normal internal chemistry that may be associated with severe tying-up.

Selenium, like many of the other trace elements, is very poisonous if the horse is fed too much. In fact, until recently it was illegal to sell feed supplements containing selenium because of the ease with which toxicity could be produced. There are now a number of preparations available for giving selenium in the feed, and you might want to consider these if your area is known to have a significant problem with selenium. Alternately, an often-used and safer approach is to give selenium by intramuscular injection once a month. These preparations also contain vitamin E, without which the selenium does not function properly. However, given the very narrow margin of safety when administering selenium by any route, it is always best to seek the advice of your veterinarian regarding such supplementation.

The exact nature of the relationship between vitamin E and selenium is not well known, even in those species where extensive research has been done. What is known is that the requirements for the two go hand-in-hand. The horse may need supplemental vitamin E if you live in a selenium deficient area or if he is consuming poor-quality hay or pasture with little or minimal grain. However, the horse does have some stores of vitamin E in his body, and these can help him to weather periods of poor forage without developing problems. For this reason, supplementation should be kept in the range of 200 to 400 IU per day for the average thousand-pound horse.

Finally, consideration must be given to the remainder of the vitamins— vitamin K, the B-vitamin complex (thiamine, riboflavin, B12, niacin, pantothenic acid, folic acid, biotin, and B6), and vitamin C.

Vitamin K

Vitamin K is manufactured by the microorganisms inhabiting the large intestine of the horse, probably in sufficient quantities to meet needs. Once absorbed, it is processed by the liver and this "activated form" of the vitamin plays a vital role in blood clotting. Clinical problems with deficiency of this vitamin, under normal conditions, are virtually unheard of. Ongoing severe intestinal upsets, or liver disease, can both increase the requirement for this vitamin and at the same time cause a decrease in the amount available. However, supplementation is administered by intramuscular injection, and this is one vitamin you will not need to worry about feeding.

The B Vitamins

The B family of vitamins contains the eight specific compounds listed above. These vitamins are involved in the normal functioning of the neurological and muscular systems and in blood production. Deficiencies can result in nervousness, muscle spasm or shakiness, personality changes, and anemia. There is also some thought that riboflavin deficiency may be involved in causing periodic ophthalmia, or "moon blindness"—a progressively blinding eye disease (see Chapter 6). It is generally assumed that the horse's intestinal bacteria manufacture enough B vitamins to meet his needs, and there are no firm guidelines for providing supplements. However, anything that interferes with the normal environment of the intestines and the activity of its bacteria can alter the production and/or absorption of these vitamins. Such influences would include diarrhea, colic from any cause, parasitism, poor-quality feed, decreased feed or water intake for any reason, and the administration of oral antibiotics. Older horses are particularly prone to suffering as a result of any or all of the above alterations. Furthermore, the effects of

Table 5

Adequate Dietary Concentrations for Vitamins and Minerals

	Maintenance	Pregnant or Lactating	Working
Sodium chloride (salt)	0.10%	0.10%	0.30%
Potassium	0.6% of the ration*		
Sulfur	0.15%	0.15%	0.15%
Iodine	0.1-0.6 mg/kg	0.1-0.6 mg/kg	0.1-0.6 mg/kg
Copper	10 mg/kg	10 mg/kg	10 mg/kg
Iron	40 mg/kg	50 mg/kg	40 mg/kg
Manganese	40 mg/kg	40 mg/kg	40 mg/kg
Zinc	40 mg/kg	40 mg/kg	40 mg/kg
Vitamin A	2,000 IU/kg	3,000 IU/kg	2,000 IU/kg
Vitamin D	300 IU/kg	600 IU/kg	300 IU/kg
Vitamin E	50 IU/kg	80 IU/kg	50 IU/kg
Vitamin K	Unknown		
Vitamin C	Unknown		
Thiamine	3 mg/kg	3 mg/kg	5 mg/kg
Riboflavin	2 mg/kg	2 mg/kg	2 mg/kg
B12	Unknown		
Niacin	Unknown		
Pantothenic acid	Unknown		
Folic acid	Unknown		
Biotin	Unknown		
Vitamin B6	Unknown		

* Adequate amounts are present in a normal diet with approximately 50% forage
** Amount present in trace mineral salt

submaximal intake of the B vitamins may be very insidious (e.g., non-specific irritability, poor appetite, mild muscle cramping) and difficult to recognize as nutritional problems.

For these reasons, it is probably advisable to feed the older horse a vitamin supplement containing the B vitamins. Try to find a supplement that contains all the B vitamins at the minimum recommended levels indicated in Table 5. It is known that the B vitamins are relatively free from any side effects or dangers, even in very large amounts, so you may be wise to choose a supplement that exceeds the minimum requirements if your horse regularly encounters problems that could lead to decreased efficiency of his intestinal tract. This will provide a margin of safety for the horse who does not always absorb things properly.

Vitamin C

Finally, there is vitamin C. This vitamin has received much publicity in recent years and has been touted as everything from a cure for the common cold to a preventative measure for cancer. In fact, there is some very sound scientific evidence behind these claims, although the truth is probably less dramatic. In addition to its contribution to optimal function of the immune system, vitamin C plays a central role in maintaining the health of tendons and ligaments. Most recently, people have been feeding vitamin C and vitamin-C-related compounds to horses who have trouble with bleeding from the lungs after heavy exercise. Many claim remarkable results with this therapy, although the reason behind the apparent success of vitamin C in controlling lung bleeding is still obscure.

In any event, there is no doubt that vitamin C is a very important element in the diet. Unfortunately, virtually nothing is known about the vitamin C requirements of the horse. What is known is that the horse does synthesize this vitamin in his body, and it has always been assumed that he does so in adequate amounts. However, given the fact that vitamin C is safe and its potential benefits are so great, it is probably advisable to supplement the diet of the aged horse with vitamin C, particularly since his natural diet is extremely low in vitamin C and he must rely on normal production in the body to meet his needs. A level of between 1.0 and 5.0 grams per day should be appropriate.

Vitamin Recommendations

Translating the information on trace elements and vitamins into a simple recommendation of what supplement to give is no simple task. The first guideline is to learn to read the labels on supplements. Those containing excessive amounts of vitamins A, D, E, or K ("excessive" being over the recommended daily requirement) should be avoided. Similarly, avoid supplements containing copper and iron; these are usually not required and could be toxic. Special care is needed with any supplement containing selenium, which also can be toxic. In fact, preparations containing any of the latter three trace elements should only be given on the specific recommendation of a veterinarian. However, zinc, vitamin C, and the B-complex vitamins are all very safe even in large quantities and are known to play critical roles in many body functions. Their levels are directly linked to the general health and efficiency of the horse's intestinal tract. Since the aged horse is most likely to suffer from intestinal upsets and to be less tolerant of any change in his feed—and in many cases it has not even been established that a normal horse can meet his requirements when feed quality is variable—supplementation with these elements is usually prudent for the older horse. Although the lack of good research in this area means that even the minimum guidelines

Table 6

Feeding the Older Horse

Condition	Hay/ 100 Lb.	Grain/ 100 Lb.	Type Feed
At Rest	1.5-2.0	0-0.5	Mixed or legume hay
Light Work, Full Turnout, Chronic Disease	1.0-2.0	0.5-1.0	Mixed or legume hay Oats or 70:30 oats:corn or 70:30 oats: barley
Medium to Heavy Work, Stress*	1.0-2.0	0.75-1.5	Mixed or legume hay Oats or 70:30 oats: corn or 70:30 oats: barley
Infection and Fever	1.0-1.25	1.0-2.0	Mixed or legume hay (prefer legume) Oats or 60-70:40-30 oats:barley or 80:30 oats:soybean or 80:20 oats:wheat bran
Pregnancy	0.75-1.5	0.75-1.5	Mixed or legume hay 80:20 oats:wheat bran or
Lactation	1.0-2.0	1.0-2.0	45:45:10 oats:barley:wheat bran or 95:5 oats: soybean

* Stress conditions include any acute illness or injury, inclement weather (primarily cold), lameness, shipping long distances, heavy training, or competition schedules

recommended in Table 5 are suspect, a horse who is receiving a good diet should not need more than the minimum daily requirements listed to give him adequate coverage. Any intestinal disorder or a condition that causes a decrease in appetite will dictate an increase in the B vitamin supplementation the horse gets.

Nutrition is an often dry and at least superficially difficult topic to master. However, nothing is more central to the health and well-being of the horse—particularly the older horse. Table 6 lists the recommended amounts of feed for adult horses performing at various levels. It must also be remembered, however, that these are only averages and may not apply to your horse. Tall but light horses, such as most Thoroughbreds or registered Quarter Horses or Appaloosas with a great deal of Thoroughbred breeding, and/or nervous animals may need much more feed, notably grain, to maintain their weight. With a little time, anyone can become familiar with the language of nutrition and learn to evaluate a feed or feed supplement by reading the breakdown provided. The result could well be a longer, happier, and more productive life for the horse.

4

Seasonal Care

*E*xtremes of weather require certain management modifications for horses of any age. However, this is particularly important for the older horse as he is less adept at handling stress in general and is likely to have some chronic problems that will aggravate and magnify those created by the weather.

WINTER

The winter months can be particularly hard on an older horse. The main problem to be considered is infectious diseases. Cold weather and chills are not sufficient in and of themselves to cause any flu or similar illness. However, these nonspecific stresses do lower the body's defenses against disease. As the horse ages, his natural immunity to infectious disease gradually declines anyway, making him a prime target in the winter for every infectious disease.

General preventative measures include limiting the horse's exposure to other horses, keeping him as warm and dry as possible, and making certain that his nutritional needs are adequately met.

Comfort

There is no need to actually quarantine the horse for the duration of the winter—and very little point to having him if you can't enjoy your normal activities. However, it certainly is wise to keep your horse away from other horses if you know he will be exposed to a disease and/or if the weather conditions are particularly bad.

Keeping the horse as warm and dry as possible does not mean swaddling him in blankets and confining him to a stall. In order to tolerate the winter, he must be accustomed to the weather changes to some extent. What this recommendation refers to are common-sense measures such as not turning the horse out in bad weather unless he has a good shelter, providing him with a good all-weather blanket (such as a lined canvas turnout blanket), and drying him off immediately if he becomes wet. Barns need not be heated, and the horse will probably remain healthier if the difference between the barn and outside is not too great. An efficient system for exchanging the air should exist to avoid a build-up of stale and humid air, which can harbor large numbers of viruses or be heavy with irritating ammonia fumes or dust. Common sense is the best guide here, the goal being an "airy" barn that has no drafts directly hitting the horse.

This 19-year-old Thoroughbred gelding, owned by Katy Finegan of Gettysburg, Pennsylvania, is shown wearing the recommended turnout canvas blanket with surcingle and leg straps.

Vaccinations

Since the older horse is more likely to come down with an infectious disease, it is wise to take particular care with his vaccination schedules (see Chapter 2, "Routine Health Care"). We cannot fully protect the horse from infectious diseases with the vaccinations available, but they do afford some protection, and proper scheduling can maximize such coverage. In particular, wintertime is the season for vaccination against rhinopneumonitis and influenza. Both are respiratory tract viruses, although rhinopneumonitis also causes abortion. The minimum recommended vaccination schedules for both diseases is once or possibly twice a year, depending upon the manufacturer. This minimum schedule is appropriate for horses who will not be likely to leave the farm during the winter and for those kept on a farm that will have minimal or no traffic of horses on and off the premises, i.e., minimum exposure. Vaccinations should be given about two weeks before the time you would normally expect the most severe winter weather to begin. If your horse will be traveling off the premises to show, hunt, or perform any activity that will expose him to other horses, or if there is normally frequent movement of horses on and off the premises during the winter, vaccination can be increased to as often as once per month in attempts to keep his antibody levels high. It is also possible to adjust the schedule to accommodate periods of anticipated exposure during only part of the winter by scheduling vaccinations for two weeks to ten days preceding an occasional show or other activity. The added cost of extra vaccinations is very minimal, particularly when compared to that of having to treat respiratory infection for an extended period.

Feed

Meeting the nutritional demands of cold weather is important to maintaining the horse's resistance to disease. It also affects how he will cope with the other problems he may encounter in colder weather. The basic adjustment to be made in winter is the provision of more calories. The horse needs this extra energy just to keep up his body weight and will begin to burn fat to keep himself warm if underfed. To meet these cold-weather needs, begin by increasing roughage, up to free choice hay. This not only provides the calories but actually generates heat within the body since hay is digested by fermentation in the large intestine and fermentation itself generates heat. If this fails, a good place to start might be to give 10 percent of the total feed ration required as grain. If the horse is already receiving this much grain, you might consider switching to more or all corn, keeping the total pounds of feed the same, to provide more calories (see Chapter 3, "Feeding the Older Horse"). If this fails, recalculate the feed requirements at 5 percent above the level needed to maintain his weight in easier weather conditions, increasing gradually as necessary. You might also want to try adding corn oil to the ration, at a rate of around 8 ounces per day, beginning with 2-ounce increments and working up gradually. Obviously, these recommendations will also have to be modified up or down depending upon the horse's activity level. If you own a field hunter or have a heavy show schedule in the winter, or if your horse is on year-round turnout, the feed demands during this season will be maximal. The best guide must always be how well the horse is maintaining his condition. Weekly use of a weight tape (which gives an estimate of the horse's weight based on his girth) will help you keep an accurate and objective eye on his needs.

Other, more general considerations related to feed include the needs to maintain a drinkable water source and to prevent grain and hay from becoming wet or frozen. Always keep in mind that the ideal is to have water available twenty-four hours a day and feed in perfect condition for as long as the horse cares to take to consume it. There may be times when it is impossible to meet this ideal, but any compromise invites colic or choke (see Chapter 7, "The Gastrointestinal Tract"). If the horse has any tendency to show digestive problems, consider switching him to a management program that will minimize or avoid such problems as frozen water or feed. Hay of some sort should be available for most of the day. This may mean using a different quality of hay that allows you to feed more, particularly if the horse is getting 100 percent alfalfa at the proper amounts. Also, a great deal of hay is lost if the horse is fed outdoors in snow or mud. It may be necessary to feed as much as 25 to 50 percent more hay than you would to a horse confined to a stall just to keep him occupied and allow for losses. The horse that only gets hay and grain once or twice a day is more likely to chew the fences and fight at feeding time. Even more important, the digestive system is designed to accommodate almost constant eating. His stomach is relatively small and cannot tolerate a day's feed all at once. Feeding in this way can lead to overeating and colic and/or colic secondary to the abnormal eating pattern.

The best approach is to feed the grain in a minimum of two meals (the more the better) and keep hay available at all times. If a hay bunker or other way to keep the hay somewhat protected is available, you may wish to offer a good-quality mixed hay twenty-four hours a day. Alternately, you should hay the horse at least three times daily, dividing up the amount you calculate he would need if fed under more controlled circumstances and supplementing this as necessary to allow for hay that is trampled or otherwise made inedible. If you are feeding alfalfa and do not wish to switch to a mixed hay, another approach would be to make up the extra hay need with a grass hay of medium to good quality. The grass hay will serve to keep the horse occupied and provide him with something in his digestive tract at all times. It will also give some extra nutrients. The majority of his needs will still be met by the alfalfa, as most horses can be counted on to consume the better hay first, thus guaranteeing a minimum loss of the good hay. Keep the grass hay available at all times, supplementing the supply up to three times a day, and feed the alfalfa when the horse is given his grain.

Lameness and Foot Care

The other major problem that often is exacerbated in the winter is lameness. Frozen ground conditions frequently aggravate chronic problems, particularly foot problems. In addition, if the horse is being used less frequently, the chances are good he is not receiving the same routine attention from the blacksmith and owner, again leading to foot problems.

The horse should be given a thorough going over for signs of soreness prior to the worst part of winter. If necessary, your veterinarian should be called to define the problem and advise you on any necessary treatments or special precautions to take with the horse. This is particularly important for the horse that is turned out in a group in the winter as feed often becomes a focal point of their day and fighting becomes more intense. The horse that is sore may be prevented from getting adequate food or water because he is too lame to compete.

Even previously sound horses can develop foot problems on frozen ground. This is particularly true if they were accustomed to wearing shoes but had them pulled for the winter. Generalized bruising and soreness is common under these conditions. You may also have trouble with more frequent abscesses and even thrush when the feet go unattended for long periods of time. Horses who remain shod may be less likely to have problems with bruising but can develop painful corns under their shoes if resetting schedules are not kept as frequent as necessary during the winter.

To prevent these problems, the horse's feet should be picked out daily if at all possible. He should also be observed at feeding times for any sign of lameness, including an apparent reluctance to join the group stampede at feeding time. The horse should be shod at the first sign of a shortened gait indicating foot tenderness. Rim or full pads should be used if simple shoeing alone is not enough to keep him comfortable. These problems are not likely to get better if shoeing is delayed, and they could lead to the horse not receiving proper nutrition.

Skin Care

Skin problems are another worry in the winter. Long winter coats often lead to moist, warm skin conditions underneath that are very favorable to bacterial and fungal growths. This is exacerbated by both exposing the horse to wet weather and by keeping him blanketed, with the most favorable conditions for skin infection occurring if he remains in a wet blanket. Also, the horse with a heavy winter coat will often be groomed less frequently, and those groomings will be less effective and complete. Once started, these skin infections, commonly known as "rain rot," are notoriously difficult to clear up, and the horse may show large, patchy, oozing bald areas in a surprisingly short period of time. The added nonspecific stress of the bad weather also makes him more likely to develop such infections and to show a decreased ability to control their spread.

The best treatment is prevention. There is no substitute for regular grooming. Heavy winter coats call for the regular and enthusiastic use of a curry comb and hard brush to lift out deep dirt and stimulate circula-

The lesions of "rain rot" begin as small, raised scabs with the overlying hair sticking up slightly.

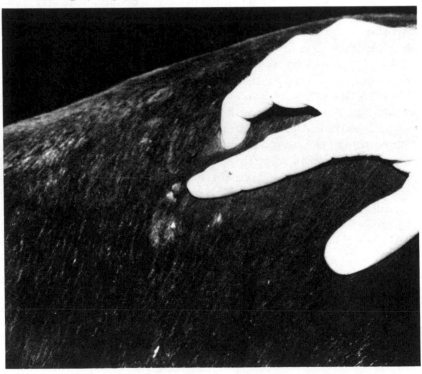

tion. This can literally take hours, particularly if your grooming is sporadic, and the best investment you can make is in a grooming vacuum that will make short work of deep dirt. If the horse is to be kept blanketed, he should have a good supply of sheets to wear underneath that can be washed easily when they become dirty or matted with hair. If he is on turnout, his outer blanket should be canvas to prevent his standing wet.

Unfortunately, even horses that are faithfully groomed may develop skin infections. If caught early, these are sometimes possible to clear up with regular baths with an iodine-containing shampoo such as Betadine. However, many cases remain resistant to this treatment as long as the winter coat is in place, with new areas of infection popping up just as you seem to be getting on top of the last. In these circumstances, the best course is to clip the horse so that local treatment can be done readily. Clipping often uncovers disease that is far more widespread than you would first expect. Once a horse is clipped, most infections will respond to the iodine shampoo treatments within seven to ten days. Resistant cases can usually be cleared by application of a final rinse containing the drug Captan, a common antifungal agent sold in nurseries and other garden supply stores. This is mixed at a rate of one tablespoon per gallon of water and applied to the horse; the excess is scraped off. The above course of treatment—clipping and bathing the affected areas daily with Betadine with or without Captan rinses—is strongly recommended for any horse who develops a skin infection on 10 percent or more of his body on first inspection. This is because the older horse with decreased immunity is unlikely to respond to more conservative measures, and the nature of these infections is such that they are difficult to clear under the best of circumstances.

SUMMER

Hot weather carries its own set of problems for the older horse. Dehydration and electrolyte disturbances head the list, with skin disease a close second.

Exercise

Most people have the sense not to overwork a horse in hot weather, and severe dehydration with electrolyte imbalance is blessedly rare when exercise is approached sensibly and the horse has free access to water and salt. It is important to remember that the older horse may have hidden problems and weaknesses of his respiratory and cardiac systems that make overwork in hot weather particularly dangerous. It is essential to avoid any conditions that would interfere with the horse's normal intake of water and salt, even if the work he is being asked to do does not seem to be extreme. For example, a long day's showing or trail riding may not call for particularly hard and fast exercise, but the horse must go for long periods without feed, water, or salt and may be forced to stand in a hot trailer for prolonged periods. Even a modest pace of work, such as a comfortable trot, can lead to overheating, dehydration, and electrolyte imbalances if carried on for several hours.

When working an aged horse in hot weather, never exceed the limits of what he has been conditioned to do under similar weather conditions. His usual workout in the spring could be too stressful in hot and humid weather. Some sweating is unavoidable—and even desirable as this is how the horse cools himsel—but he should not be worked to the point that a lather forms. Similarly, work always involves a rise in heart rate, respiratory rate, and body temperature, but his pulse and breathing should return to levels not exceeding twice normal in three to five minutes and temperature to near normal (no greater than 100 degrees) in the same time period. You should be thoroughly familiar with your horse's normal resting pulse, respiratory rate, and temperature and use these to guide you in working him. Respiratory rates and temperatures are simple to obtain, although it is often difficult to feel the pulse, particularly if the horse is agitated and moving around. In these circumstances it may be easier for you to determine the heart rate by sliding your hand under his left elbow to feel the pulse (see photograph on page 119).

Special care should be given to adequately warming up and cooling down the aged horse. A good general guideline is ten minutes of strong walking before and after any work. The cool-down walking may be interrupted at the five-minute mark to evaluate the breathing, heart rate, and temperature. When you have finished walking, remove all tack and sponge or hose the horse off with cool water. He may then be given access to hay and water as long as he is not consuming more than a half bucket or so (one to two gallons) of water at any one time. If his thirst seems greater than this, allow him to have no more than half a bucket and then offer the same amount at fifteen- to twenty-minute intervals until he is satisfied. Horses who do not recover to acceptable pulse, respiration, or temperature should be given only sips of water at five- to ten-minute intervals until they have returned to normal. Unrestricted access to water may result in colic and even founder as the blood normally supplying the intestines is busy at work in the muscles until the horse is properly cooled out.

No shortcuts should be taken in cooling out any horse, particularly an aged horse. It is known from other species that even very athletically active individuals can suffer from sudden death if they work hard and stop suddenly. This can happen even when the cardiovascular system is perfectly normal; however, the changes in circulatory and cardiac efficiency accompanying aging make the tolerance to such sudden changes in activity even more dangerous.

The practice of feeding electrolyte supplements or adding salt to the water are discussed in detail in Chapter 3. It should be mentioned here, however, that the horse that is working regularly and hard in hot weather may be a candidate for electrolyte replacement. This is particularly true with any type of endurance work. However, electrolyte mixtures should be given only on the advice of a veterinarian. Addition of salt or other mixtures to the feed should be avoided. When an electrolyte-laced water source is offered, it is imperative to ensure that the horse always has free access to untreated water as well. Finally, everyone potentially involved in the care of the horse should be well-instructed in the proper way to prepare the mixture and know that the horse must also have fresh water. Buckets should be clearly labelled, or of different colors, and a note should be posted on the stall door as extra precautions. Failure to observe these precautions can lead to dehydration and electrolyte imbalances even worse than those caused by the work.

Skin Problems

The summer months are commonly associated with a variety of difficult-to-treat skin problems. Among the worst of these is onchocerciasis. This is a condition characterized by hair loss, crusting, scaling, swelling, redness, and open oozing areas on the ventral midline (belly) and sometimes on the face. It is caused in most cases by the immature forms of a parasite, *Onchocerca cervicalis,* that in its innocuous adult form is transmitted to horses via biting insects and inhabits the large ligament on the top of the neck. This parasite produces tremendous numbers of immature forms, called microfilaria, that then travel in the tissues under the skin and set up irritation in the areas mentioned. Most cases are also complicated by irritation from flies attracted to oozing areas of flesh and by secondary bacterial infection.

Treatment proceeds on two levels: controlling the population of microfilaria and combatting the secondary problems of infection and fly irritation. There is no way to permanently eliminate the microfilaria as the adult is protected and will continue to produce them. The circulating microfilaria, however, can be killed periodically by administration of diethylcarbamazine, a drug used also to kill immature forms of heartworm in dogs. Your veterinarian will recommend an appropriate dosage schedule for this drug. It is also often advisable to treat the horse with steroids, antihistamines, or other agents during the first few days of diethylcarbamazine treatment, as killing off large numbers of the microfilaria can cause severe allergic reactions. This parasite may also invade the eye and be responsible for "moon blindness" or periodic ophthalmia (see Chapter 6), and the death of large numbers of larvae in the eye could result in serious inflammation and even blindness. In fact, the presence of obvious eye changes may be a contraindication to treatment with diethylcarbamazine at some times.

The secondary problems are controlled by cleansing the affected areas with plain or antibacterial soaps and removing all crusts. An antibacterial cream, sometimes containing steroids, is then applied, and fly repellent is used generously around the edges of the area. The area should be attended to at least twice daily (more frequent treatments are often necessary early in the treatment). If the horse is on turnout and/or if it is difficult to have someone treat him this often, it is best to move him to other quarters where he can be treated aggressively, at least for the first week or so, to allow for the condition to be controlled. Similarly, if flies are a great problem, it may be necessary to arrange to have him stabled until the open areas of flesh are healed. In fact, flies can be such a problem that some cases of midline dermatitis appear to be caused by flies alone. Investment in a long-lasting fly repellent, such as a gel from your veterinarian, is essential to the well-being of any animal kept on turnout in the summer months.

Another problem in the summer is habronemiasis—"summer sores." This is a huge, granulating infection, often on the back of the pasterns, caused by infection of a break in the skin with the larvae of the stomach worm habronema. The eggs of this parasite are ingested by flies and mature to the larval stage within the fly. Open wounds become infected when larvae emerge from flies that are feeding on them. The treatment involves tubing the horse with one of the organophosphate wormers and topically applying an ointment containing the same drug.

"Scratches," or "grease heel," is another skin problem in the pastern area that particularly plagues horses kept on turnout. It is an infection of the skin that follows small scratches from rough grasses, burrs, or twigs. In severe cases, the entire leg to the knee can swell, and the small vessels that carry lymphatic fluid can become involved and scarred, leading to a permanently swollen leg. Horses with long hair at the fetlock and pastern are particularly prone to severe infections. Treatment involves clipping and cleansing the involved areas with an application of a drying wound powder to the area. Ointments and sprays should generally be avoided. It is best to prevent this problem from ever occurring by clipping the lower legs of "hairy" horses and inspecting horses regularly to detect and treat small skin breaks. Regular mowing and removal of burrs or other irritating plants from the horse's pasture are also advisable.

Also, in summer horses may develop bacterial and fungal infections as described under winter problems. This is usually a problem with horses on constant turnout that get repeatedly soaked with rain and are rarely groomed. Treatment is as described previously.

The summer months are also the time for sunburn in light-skinned horses such as Appaloosas or palominos and for a wide range of allergic reactions characterized by bumps or even open areas on the skin. The only way to avoid sunburn is to keep the horse out of the sun, although you may wish to try sunscreens or zinc oxide ointment (the white cream that lifeguards use) on sensitive areas when the horse is turned out or worked. Most allergic reactions are caused by insect bites, and again investment in a long-lasting gel insect repellent is essential.

The seasonal problems of older horses are much the same as for younger animals. However, as with all management questions in caring for aged horses, special care must be taken in consideration of their decreased resistance to disease and increased susceptibility to stress in general. Anything that interferes with the nutrition or water and electrolyte balance of the aged horse is likely to have far more serious consequences than with younger and more resilient animals. Finally, constant turnout and/or long periods of time without regular handling put the aged horse at higher risk for developing many seasonal health problems. Every effort must be made to prevent problems or to catch them in the early stages.

5

Conditioning

Horses may be worked at virtually any sport you can imagine well into their twenties, although some loss of speed and/or chronic lameness and medical problems usually dictate some modification of their activities. There are as many different conditioning and training regimens as there are activities, each specially suited to the work involved. However, there are some basic recommendations concerning conditioning the older horse that should be applied in all cases to provide for safe training and maintenance of an athletically active aged horse.

The process of aging results in decreased lean body mass (muscle). Tendons are not as adaptable as they lose elasticity. Muscles may sag as the ligaments they are attached by weaken. The process of repair and remodeling critical to athletic performance may be limited by increased requirements for key nutrients in the face of decreased absorption. However, regular exercise will help minimize these problems.

Rule number one is that if you want the horse to continue to be active, it is best (and sometimes imperative) never to completely "let him down." This means avoidance of long periods of inactivity. Although stall rest is particularly disastrous, even turnout can lead to a significant loss of condition depending upon the horse's personality and the conditions of the turnout.

When horses are not regularly exercised they lose their physical conditioning at variable rates, depending upon the individual animal and how fit he was when work stopped. Most horses out of work for a month or

"Dream Weaver" is a 19-year-old bay Thoroughbred gelding, 15.3 hands, owned by Alice Bennett of Park Forest, Illinois. Out of eight classes at the Lake County, Indiana, county fair, "Dream Weaver" placed third, fourth, fifth (twice), and sixth. Photograph by Jack Greene, Murfreesboro, Tennessee.

longer, particularly aged horses, will probably need to start their training over again to regain their strength and flexibility, although the shorter periods of lay-up may not be associated with a total loss of cardiovascular fitness. When the time off stretches to several months, a year, or longer, it may not be possible to return the horse to his original level of fitness, or even to train him to the point he would have been able to achieve if work had not been stopped. This is unlikely to be a significant problem for the pleasure horse, or even many show horses, although it is often found that they will take longer to condition than when younger. However, for the field hunter, event horse, endurance horse, or horse used for any other activity that is more strenuous, a long lay-off may mean that the horse can no longer compete as often or as well as he did before and/or will be plagued by injuries that are directly related to his inability to reach the physical level required to handle the stress of such work.

Horses who are routinely given the winter off will begin to show the above effects as they approach late middle age (around fifteen years old and older) on the average. This problem will also be compounded if there are any chronic lameness problems related to arthritis as time completely off often results in joint stiffness that may be irreversible. If at all possible, every effort should be made to provide structured exercise two or three times during the week in the off season, even if this only amounts to longeing the horse in a field for fifteen minutes. This at least will help to maintain his flexibility in a general way and to prevent permanent stiffening of the joints. If the horse does start to stiffen up even with this longeing schedule, you will have to make arrangements to work him longer and/or more often. When in doubt as to exactly what measures to take, consult your veterinarian.

Whether time off has been one month or one year, resumption of training is best accomplished by using the principles of interval training, as discussed in detail on pages 78–82.

When any horse stops active training and exercising, his muscles lose tone, ligaments and tendons shorten and lose some elasticity, and the cardiopulmonary system becomes decompensated, i.e., loses its ability to handle the increased demands of exercise. There are many complicated biochemical, structural, and physiological mechanisms at work here; however, the point to remember is that such deterioration is inevitable and the older horse may never again return to his previous level of fitness. With younger adult horses in heavy training, such as racing, a good rule of thumb is that the horse will be set back two to three days in his training schedule for every day of inactivity after the initial two to three days. This figure can also be applied to the older horse, but represents only a minimum estimate of how long it will take to recondition the horse. As an example, if you own a field hunter and are forced to confine him to stall rest for ten days in the middle of the hunting season (for example, to treat a foot abscess), it will take a minimum of two to three weeks of conditioning for him to return to the level of fitness he exhibited prior to the lay-up.

These minimum times are often prolonged by a general decrease in the ease with which the horse regains his muscle tone, by a decline in elasticity of his tendons and ligaments, by a loss of flexibility in his joints, by aging of the cardiovascular system, and by limitations and complications arising from chronic lameness or medical illnesses. The horse of ten who has remained reasonably active throughout his life may require no special considerations, but advancing age from this point on is correlated with increased difficulty in achieving physical fitness, with setbacks secondary to soreness or stiffness increasingly encountered. It helps to remember that one "horse-year" is roughly equal to three "human-years" (assuming life expectancies of twenty-five and seventy-five years, respectively). The thirty-year-old human who has remained fit can continue to perform without any noticeable difficulties, although he or she may no longer be competitive with younger athletes. However, by the age of sixty (the 20-year-old horse) capacity for exercise may very well be limited by the effects of age itself and those imposed by any chronic illnesses or injuries.

The horse with chronic degenerative arthritis is particularly difficult to bring back as forced inactivity will often result in loss of flexibility. This type of horse will seem as sound, or perhaps even sounder, after the lay-up period as he was before it, but he commonly develops pain when you try to bring him back. The regular exercise he had enjoyed previously was keeping blood flow at a maximal level and providing for flexibility and strength of the muscles and the tendons and ligaments that provide support to the joints. The continuous exercise was also probably preventing the formation of restricting calcium deposits simply by keeping the joint moving. After his rest period, the loss of good supporting strength and flexibility may make the joint movement uncontrolled, resulting in pain. Stiffness that is secondary to calcium deposition during the rest period may prove to be irreversible. Finally, the loss of conditioning can lead to early tiring, which, combined with pain, makes missteps more likely, leading to possible further injury to the arthritic joint or to other areas. The longer the period of inactivity, the worse these problems are likely to be.

The presence of chronic medical problems also complicates conditioning of the aged horse. A good example is "heaves" or chronic respiratory disease. When the horse is fit, his oxygen demands at rest and during exercise are less than when he is out of condition, and his body is more efficient at meeting those needs. The horse with a chronic respiratory disease may very well have requirements that exceed those of an otherwise normal horse, but he can meet these easier when he is fit. When the horse stops being conditioned, he loses the beneficial efficiency his regular exercise schedule had maintained. He may also suffer from increased damage due to the continual progression of his disease. When he loses his fitness, it may even become more difficult for him to breathe at rest if the previous cardiovascular conditioning had been helping him to maintain a certain level of air exchange. The result is difficult respiration, which in and of itself can cause damage to the lung. A heavey horse not kept in condition may very easily lose not only his ability to exercise comfortably but also his efficiency at getting enough air at rest. This leads to labored breathing and higher pressures within the lung that cause yet more damage. Add to this the changes he would be expected to show in any case simply because his disease is one that progresses over time.

Attempts to restore this horse to his previous level of fitness can be extremely difficult (if not impossible) and require a great deal of patience and long, slow work.

EVALUATING PROBLEMS

The first step to devising a safe and effective work schedule to regain or maintain conditioning is to take inventory of any problems the horse has. This should include the directly involved problems with lameness or cardiopulmonary disease, as well as nonspecific factors such as difficulty in holding weight or chronic colic. This last-mentioned category of problems must be included since the older horse (as any horse) should always be viewed as a whole, with all aspects of his care interrelated. The most carefully devised training schedule will be worthless if he cannot or will not take in enough feed to allow for that level of activity.

After you have formed your problem list, you should view each item as to its possible negative effect on exercise. For example, a mild case of heaves may only be a problem for you in hot, humid summer weather and possibly not even then if the horse is in good condition at the time. If the goal with such a horse includes a heavy schedule of activity in the summer, allow for sufficient conditioning time so that he is near maximal condition by late spring. If the horse is known to have navicular disease or some other chronic lameness, you may anticipate problems at virtually any stage of his training but most likely during the periods of heaviest or fastest work. Again, the training schedule should allow for him to reach the proper level of conditioning well in advance of the time you will want to use him to allow for the correction of any problems and setbacks in his schedule. Your veterinarian may be able to advise you as to the problems and early warning signs you should expect when dealing with a horse that has chronic problems, when to expect them, and whether or not your expectations for the horse are realistic.

An example of just how much can be accomplished with proper individualized training is the story of "Boff." "Boff" was a twelve-year-old Argentinean Thoroughbred stallion with a very interesting history. He had been raced in South America as a young horse but around the age of five developed a hind-end lameness that was never really diagnosed but prevented him from training or racing. He was retired to stud where he did well for several years until he began to have decreasing sperm counts and was once again out of a job.

An American saw the horse and bought him as a show prospect on looks alone. Early training showed he did have tremendous potential for jumping and was an excellent mover. However, very early on in his training the old hind-end lameness problem reappeared. He would have days when he performed normally, while on other days, usually when schooling was heavy, he would suddenly and for no apparent reason stop dead in his tracks.

By this time the horse was a ten-year-old and his value for resale had started to decline. When no obvious cause of his problem was found, he was given away to a girl who hoped he would be able to tolerate dressage work.

She turned "Boff" out for the winter, hoping this would improve his problem. The next spring she noted he had lost quite a bit of muscling over his hindquarters, more so than elsewhere on his body. When she started training him, with trotting and cantering in the ring, he quickly started to show the old pattern of stopping dead. He even seemed incapable of trotting briskly or cantering.

This 16-year-old Morgan stallion, "Con Man," tied for Reserve Champion in the AHSA/Insilco Zone I awards at Fourth Level with rider/owner Susan Woods, proving the older horse can truly be competitive. Photograph by Susan Sexton.

The first impression was that the horse was suffering from a general loss of muscle conditioning from the prolonged turnout and might be tying up as well. However, blood tests for muscle damage were negative. A complete lameness examination, with X-rays, was also negative. Then a rectal examination was done, and this revealed that the large arteries supplying the hind end were thickened and hard, findings characteristic of long-term strongyle ("bloodworm") damage. He was receiving just enough blood to his hind end for rest or very light exercise. Any higher demands caused severe pain that would have a sudden onset and be relieved within a few minutes of stopping work.

With this in mind, the first step for his owner was to define his limitations. It was discovered that he could tolerate walking on the flat or on hills with no problems at all, so his conditioning program began with walks of two miles, working up to ten miles. He handled this very well and began to regain some muscle bulk. However, when his owner tried to start days of ring work he would invariably stop after a few minutes of trotting.

She did discover, however, that he could do the trotting work without problems if he was walked for a minimum of two miles first. Apparently this warmup improved the circulation to his legs sufficiently that the vessels recruited during this walk period could then expand to handle the increased demand of trotting. By keeping religiously to a schedule that included a two-mile walk before any other work, his owner was able to gradually increase his periods of trotting until he was trotting easily for as long as she desired. Within two months cantering work was started, and he handled this without any difficulties as well.

"Boff" did very well in dressage competition once the key to his training was uncovered, and when his owner decided to try her luck at eventing he rose to this occasion as well when trained on an interval schedule. "Boff" has been able to compete successfully at the Preliminary level. The only special consideration his owner makes for him is that two-mile warmup before every phase. She sometimes even stays on him between phases if the break is only an hour or less. This extra activity has not affected his competitiveness in the least—not a bad ending for a horse who was retired to breeding at the age of five!

INTERVAL TRAINING

The actual creation of a training schedule obviously depends upon the activity. However, there are certain principles that should be applied to all disciplines. In general, a training protocol that is based upon the concept of interval training is the most applicable to older horses. With interval training, initial long, slow periods of work serve to lay the foundation of good muscle tone and conditioning of the tendons and ligaments.

This phase is essential to preventing injuries, which almost always result from the horse becoming fatigued.

A horse that has been performing no formal exercise at all will need a minimum of six weeks of long, slow work before progressing on to the more rigorous demands of his discipline. This is true for the dressage horse, the barrel horse, the endurance horse, or any other horse you can think of. Basic conditioning for all groups is the same: a steady progression from walking on the flat, to walking on hilly ground, to trotting on the flat, to trotting up and down hills. The amount of time to be spent at each level can only be determined by how easily the horse accomplishes the work.

Walking Phase

A common starting point might be two to four miles of walking. This will take anywhere from thirty to forty-five minutes to complete and should be done at a strong, steady walk—not poking along with frequent breaks to nibble the grass. This may not seem like much work, but the horse who is out of condition will probably show light sweating and mildly elevated pulse and respiratory rates, all of which show the walking is helping to restore him to condition. (Anyone who feels this is too little work to make a difference should try walking along beside the horse instead of riding him!) If the horse performs this activity comfortably, keep him at this level, possibly increasing to six to ten miles on level ground, for one week or so. If he is having trouble, as evidenced by an obviously increased respiratory rate or heavy sweating, remain walking on the flat until he handles this easily. Even severely unfit older horses can usually adjust to this level of activity within a total period of ten days. If he is still having problems, a veterinary examination is in order.

As a general rule, the horse who has had a prolonged period of inactivity prior to resuming training, or one with a known lameness problem of any sort, should probably be given a generous initial period of walking, increasing the distances by one-half to one mile per day whenever he is handling his previous level of activity without signs of stress. If such a horse is gradually advanced to the ten-mile mark in walking on level ground, he will have achieved a good start on cardiovascular fitness as well as strengthening of the muscles and ligaments while remaining flexible. A brisk walk of this distance is probably just as likely to produce signs of soreness as would a shorter work at the trot, but the degree of any injury will be less severe than might be the case if it were activated under the greater concussive forces of trotting. This prolonged initial walking stage is strongly recommended for any horse over the age of fifteen, even if he had no prior history of lameness problems.

Walking on Hills

The next step is walking on hills. Work up and down hills places a significantly greater load on the horse's bones, ligaments, joints, and muscles, and walking up hills even calls for greater efficiency of his cardiovascular system. If the horse was badly out of shape, the added burden will be immediately obvious. A good starting point is two to four miles of work on hilly ground and an additional one to two miles of flat walking. Work may be increased at the rate of half a mile of hill work every two or three days as the horse handles this well, up to six to eight miles on hills with the one to two miles of flat walking divided between the beginning and the end of his work. Ten to fourteen days of hill walking, on a gradually increasing schedule, will work wonders in getting the horse's cardiovascular system off to a good start and will greatly help strengthen muscles and improve the flexibility of joints and tendons. Although these long periods of walking are admittedly often boring, they give the maximum benefits with the minimum stress, a prime consideration with older horses.

When you begin hill work, you will often find that lameness problems will begin to appear. However, these are likely to be minimal at this stage, and it is often possible to continue the work, perhaps on a decreased schedule or with the help of a short period of medication, and have the horse progress to being sound again. You should not become discouraged if soreness appears at this early stage. It indicates that you would have had problems somewhere along the line in any event. The careful progression of work can lead to early uncovering of problem areas—at a stage where they can probably be managed quite effectively. The horse can then progress to more demanding work without a significant setback.

Trotting on the Flat

When the walking has been handled successfully and the horse has remained sound, it is time to add trotting on the flat. Again, the trot should be a good, strong working trot if there is to be any benefit over walking. Trotting is the beginning of serious conditioning of the cardiovascular system and also increases the strain on the horse's joints, muscles, tendons, and ligaments. Total work levels should be around two to four miles, with trotting introduced gradually. For example, day one might be: a one-mile walk, a half-mile trot, another one-mile walk, another half-mile trot (all on the flat), and two miles of hill walking. As conditioning progresses, the goal is to decrease the duration of flat and hill walking and replace it with work at the trot until finally the horse is performing the majority of his work at the trot with short recovery periods at the walk in between. A sample might be: a quarter-mile flat walk, a quarter-

At the age of 23, this Thoroughbred gelding named "Bantry" won two
seconds, a fourth, and a seventh in four novice events; was on the
second-place stadium team at a Pony Club rally; was second in a
steeplechase; and completed a hunter pace. No one would ever guess
his age from his looks!

mile hill walk, a half-mile flat trot, a quarter-mile hill walk, a half-mile flat trot, a quarter-mile hill walk, a three-quarter-mile flat trot, a quarter-mile hill walk, a half-mile flat trot, a quarter-mile hill walk, and a quarter-mile flat walk.

Judging Stress

After wading through the suggested list of intervals, you may feel the system of interval training is overly complicated. However, the basic principles are easy to understand. Goals are to gradually increase the duration of the most demanding work (the trot) and to allow for short recovery periods in between that give the horse a break but are not long enough for him to return to a completely normal pulse or respiratory rate. There are those who carry interval training to the extreme of electronically monitoring the pulse and respiration rates and setting exact criteria to be used in judging the appropriate length of the slow and hard work periods. However, for most it is sufficient to become good at judging in a rough way how much the horse is being stressed.

Specifically, your veterinarian may advise that you limit the severity of work to a 50 percent increase in the horse's respiratory rate. With practice, you can become adept at counting his respirations from his back during the walk periods. If the breathing is above the recommended level and remains there for longer than two minutes, you should cut back on the duration of the faster and/or harder work until he is comfortably handling it. If he recovers very quickly or never reaches the maximum increase you have set, increase the duration of the harder work. Also, the slower and easier work should be stopped and the harder work started again as soon as the horse's respiratory rate begins to return to normal.

As work increases beyond the stage of trotting on the flat, more generous limits may be set as to how hard the horse can work, judged by his respiratory rate or pulse. There is no way to give any reliable guidelines here (e.g., maximum acceptable respiratory rate of X per minute) as each horse, and most particularly each aged horse, must be evaluated as an individual and given limits that correspond to his soundness and general medical condition.

Your veterinarian can assist you in determining what is a safe level of stress for your horse's age and any associated problems. For example, it is known that the heart rate of the horse is in the neighborhood of 200 beats per minute during the most stressful portions of a race, while a rate of 100 to 120 might be considered a good working pulse level during conditioning. However, if your horse is over approximately fifteen years of age, or has known or suspected cardiac or lung compromise, it may be advised that you restrict the initial efforts to a pulse rate of around 80 (or twice the average resting pulse of many horses) to be safe. The choice of how you monitor the horse (by pulse or respiration or both) will be influenced partly by what is most convenient for you and partly by what is felt to be the most important parameter for your animal. For example, a horse with heaves may reach an unacceptable respiratory rate long before his pulse enters the danger zone.

If the horse plateaus at any stage of training, continuing to show signs that he is being stressed significantly but does not seem to be able to become accustomed to the work and progress, more detailed investigations are in order.

A common cause of exercise intolerance is pain. Pain will elevate pulse and respiratory rates beyond what you would expect for the level of exercise, as will anxiety about pain—whether real or anticipated. In this instance, the horse will probably also provide behavioral clues. He will be disinterested to obviously resistant to work and may develop vices such as refusing to move, balking, bucking, or rearing.

Musculoskeletal pain is an obvious possibility and a thorough lameness examination is in order. This should include a close and detailed evaluation of the back, shoulders, and neck as well as lower legs.

Other possible sources of pain include problems in the chest or abdomen. Although relatively rare as a category, they are much more likely to be found in aged horses. Pain from a large abscess in either location is a possibility (see page 109–10). Large tumors can also make the horse uncomfortable with exercise. If the horse has had abdominal surgery in the past, adhesions (scar tissue) in the abdomen may be pulled and stretched during exercise, causing pain.

If pain from these sources can be ruled out, the horse may simply be being overworked, or advanced too quickly. One clue to this will be found in the levels of muscle enzymes in his blood. Blood should be checked for SGOT (serum glutamic oxaloacetic transaminase), an indicator of recent muscle stress, as well as CPK (creatine phosphokinase), a sensitive indicator of current muscle stress/damage. The CPK level should be drawn approximately one hour after a routine exercise session, as it will peak by this time then rapidly begin to decline. You must alert your veterinarian in advance if you desire these tests since CPK is a sensitive enzyme. Serum must be separated from the blood cells as soon as blood clots and serum samples kept cool until they reach the laboratory to obtain valid test results.

Trotting on Hills

The advent of trotting on hills marks the start of what can be considered truly stressful work. In many ways, the conditioning from trotting

Owner Joanne Conley Small credited exercise over the expansive rolling hills of her turn-out field for helping to keep 21-year-old Thoroughbred mare Freeway in condition over winter lay-offs. A special memorandum goes to "Freeway". She had to be humanely destroyed on April 8, 1992. We agree with her owner that she (and other valiant older horses) "deserves to be famous" and we have no doubt that you will indeed "always love her."

on hills exceeds that of flat work at higher speeds. The cardiovascular system may have to work as hard to get the horse up a hill trotting as it would for him to gallop at moderate speeds on the flat. Trotting hills also demands maximal use of the muscles, particularly the hindquarter muscles, which results in great flexibility and strength of the joints and supporting structures, all without the damaging pounding of work at higher speeds. In fact, hill work places such demands on the muscles and joints that your horse may develop problems—notably in the hind-quarters, stifles, and hocks—that would not appear with flat work at speed unless the horse were doing a good deal of jumping or sharp turning. Again, the problems will appear relatively early in the course of his training and before any serious damage is likely to have occurred, thus allowing for diagnosis and treatment at the most desirable stage for continued work. If your horse has a history of hind-end lameness problems or any other severe lameness and you only anticipate doing flat work or light jumping in the ring with him, it is best to seek your veterinarian's advice before progressing to trotting hills as this could be placing an unnecessary stress on that particular horse. You may be advised to avoid this work.

Trotting on hills is integrated into the interval schedule just as trotting was—by substituting the work for less demanding activities and gradually increasing the duration of hill trotting compared to the less stressful activities in between. You can be flexible during any given workout with interval training, decreasing the most stressful periods if the horse is not handling them as well as expected or lengthening them and substituting more demanding intervals between the hill trots (e.g., going to trotting on the flat or hill walks instead of walks on the flat) when he is doing exceptionally well.

The total time period necessary for the horse to make the transition from walking two to four miles on the flat to performing four to eight miles of intervals including trotting on hills with ease will probably be a minimum of six weeks. At this point, his intervals would have been increased at half-mile to one-mile increments until his interval schedule would look like this: a quarter-mile flat walk, a quarter-mile hill walk, a half-mile flat trot, a half-mile hill trot, a quarter-mile hill walk, a three-quarter-mile flat trot, a quarter-mile hill trot, a quarter-mile hill walk, a three-quarter-mile hill trot, a quarter-mile flat trot, a quarter-mile hill walk, a three-quarter-mile hill trot, a half-mile flat trot, a quarter-mile hill walk, a quarter-mile flat walk. The precise length of the intervals of stressful work and "rest" or decreased work load will vary with the individual animal and may even vary from day to day for the same horse. It is important to maintain flexibility and keep in mind that the goal of interval training is to get the maximum benefit with the minimum stress on the horse. This translates into gradually increasing the length and difficulty of the inter-

This 20-year-old Appaloosa gelding, "Yankee Clipper," owned by Caroline Berry of Zebulon, North Carolina, is an excellent example of how regular and varied exercise maintains joint flexibility and muscle tone.

vals but always stopping at the predetermined pulse or respiratory rate and allowing the horse to continue working at a lower level until he is once again in the safe range. The more difficult level of activity is resumed before he has had time to completely recover down to his resting pulse or respiratory rates.

Those horses blessedly without any problems may complete this phase in as little as four weeks, as judged by how their pulse and respiration responds to the work. However, it is advisable to keep all horses on interval training of this type for a minimum of six weeks as it takes this long for the tendons and ligaments to become fully conditioned. The horse may seem extremely fit and ready to take on the world before this time as his muscles are the easiest system to condition and the muscular strength is what makes him feel good. He may even become a little difficult to handle and "full of himself." Nevertheless, always allow for the minimum of six weeks of ground work to allow for strengthening of the bones, ligaments, tendons, and joints. Shortcuts may invite lameness later on.

MAINTAINING CONDITION

As the horse approaches the end of his initial interval-training period, a decision will have to be made as to how to maintain this conditioning and progress with more specific tasks. The routine exercise schedule you use will depend to a great deal on what the horse will be doing. For example, an endurance horse or field hunter will require long works between periods of active competition or hunting, the actual duration determined by experience but probably in the neighborhood of at least ten miles per day (or every other day—see page 84); however, the speed of his works need not and should not be excessive as this only adds to the stress on his legs and is not really necessary for horses that do not compete at top speeds. On the other hand, horses who are actively racing or eventing will usually need some speed work, although this should be done on an interval schedule (e.g., half-mile speed works with a brief break in between rather than a mile at full speed). Interval speed training is just as effective as working the horse at top speed for the entire distance— e.g., a half-mile gallop, a quarter-mile trot, and a half-mile gallop can be used instead of galloping for a full mile straight—but places less strain on the legs and cardiopulmonary system. Finally, those horses in less strenuous pursuits, such as showing or pleasure hacking, will maintain their condition if worked approximately three times per week at the activity the rider enjoys. If it is known in advance that the horse will have to perform longer or harder than usual, it is best to build him up for this by increasing his training over a two- to three-week period until it approximates the level at which he will be performing.

*This 17-year-old Standardbred gelding has provided his owner,
Brooke Gaiser of Sarasota, Florida, with many years of enjoyment.
"Nyteflyte" hunts, events, competes in dressage, and even drives! As
Brooke puts it, "He's my good pal."*

*"Whimbrel," a 19-year-old American Quarter Horse, has hunted,
whipped, and hacked. He is also an excellent country pleasure
driving horse. Here, "Whimbrel" is competing in the marathon at the
Lorenzo Driving Competition in Cazenovia, New York, with his
owner, Mrs. R. James Hubbard, whip.*

Shown here is "Wynnewood Symphony," age 20, owned by Bobbi Groover, member of the Mill Creek Hunt, Wadsworth Illinois, putting in a Reserve Champion Field Hunter performance.

Many adult horses can be adequately maintained on a schedule of working every other day (three to four days per week) rather than exercising daily, particularly if they are turned out in between, even for only an hour or two a day. This corresponds well to experience with human athletes and other species of animals. How well this works for the individual horse can only be determined by trial and error; an every-other-day schedule may or may not be sufficient work for horses that only put out a top effort several times a month. On the other hand, horses who are regularly hunting two to three times per week rarely if ever need additional work unless they miss one or more hunts, at which time the longer interval work described on page 80 should be substituted for the missed hunt(s).

To summarize, there are no magic formulas for training in any discipline. All horses need an initial period of conditioning that tones their muscles and strengthens ligaments, joints, and tendons. This phase should be approximately the same regardless of the sport you follow. Interval training schedules work best for the older horse as they result in the maximum benefit from a minimum strain on the legs and cardiovascular system. Specific training for your type of activity, and schedules to maintain appropriate fitness, will be dictated by the sport and must be individualized to each horse. However, it may be possible to maintain fitness on an every-other day work schedule. The keys to successful conditioning of the aged horse are to take it slow but avoid any shortcuts to fitness. Stressing the horse too quickly could cause setbacks, but failure to provide him with a solid foundation can set the stage for fatigue and injury. When in doubt, always seek the advice of your veterinarian or a trainer you trust.

PART II

Special Problems Of Older Horses

6
Vision

ging does not seem to be associated with any particular visual problems in the horse, but there are a number of conditions that worsen over time and become troublesome in the older animal.

CATARACTS

Cataracts in other species are associated in a general way with aging and also with a number of metabolic diseases, such as diabetes. As with many such old-age diseases, not enough horses reach truly advanced age to state with certainty how significant a problem this could be. The horse does not seem to have these nonspecific aging changes though, and definitely has a low incidence of diseases like diabetes. However, cataracts can also form if the lens of the eye is traumatized. This can even occur with a blow to the head that loosens the attachments of the lens. Once the lens has been damaged, the process of cataract formation is begun. These cataracts are a type of scar that forms very slowly. An aged horse may begin to show visual problems that date back many years to a forgotten injury or other inflammatory condition in the eye.

There is no treatment for cataracts in the older horse. Surgical removal of the lens has been tried but has not been very successful in older horses as the surgery itself can cause inflammation that is even more damaging. Some horses will regain sight at least partially when the cataract

Figure 6, Normal Eye, Side View

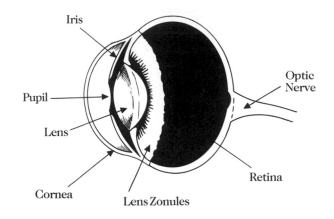

Figure 7

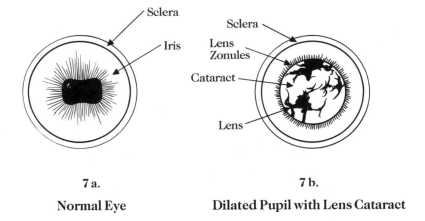

7 a.

Normal Eye

7 b.

Dilated Pupil with Lens Cataract

"matures" or "ripens," as the scarred lens will shrink and allow light to pass around its edges.

Cataracts are diagnosed by examining the eye with an ophthalmoscope or even a small flashlight. They are seen as white areas in the middle of the eye, inside the lens (see Figure 7b). Many horses normally have a Y-shaped cataract that is present from birth and does not interfere with vision. There is also a syndrome of hereditary cataracts in horses, but animals with this condition usually develop the changes at a very early age and are severely handicapped or blind by the time they are year-lings. When a cataract is discovered in an older horse, it is important to obtain as detailed a history as possible. This will help to determine if it has been present since an early age (and therefore not likely to be the cause of a new problem with vision) or can be traced to some insult to the eye or head later in life. This, together with the examination of the eye over several months, will then aid the veterinarian in determining if the cataract is likely to worsen, remain the same, or perhaps shrink and result in somewhat better vision. Since there is no treatment, a decision must be made between euthanizing the horse with severe visual changes or attempting to manipulate his environment so that he can live rela-tively happily and safely.

GLAUCOMA

Glaucoma is a condition of increased pressure within the eye, charac-terized by increased intraocular fluid, bulging eyes, and pain. Primary (unexplained) glaucoma is not a significant problem in horses, although the incidence of this problem increases with age in other species. Sec-ondary glaucoma is the result of any disease process that blocks the nor-mal flow of fluid within the eye. It is a very real possibility with any se-vere injury to the eye of a horse, most notably those involving the lens or a puncture wound.

The fluid inside the eye gives it its shape and supplies nutrition. It is formed by a tiny structure inside the eye and normally circulates from the front of the eye and back through the pupil. Any process that causes inflammation in the eye or blocks the flow of fluid through the pupil can interfere with drainage of this fluid, which then builds up causing increased pressure, pain, and eventual blindness if the condition is not recognized in time.

Among the conditions resulting in secondary glaucoma are periodic ophthalmia ("moon blindness"), penetrating wounds that cause deep in-fections, displacement of the lens, or complications of cataracts. Peri-odic ophthalmia will be discussed in detail later. The mechanism of glau-coma in this case is usually swelling that blocks drainage of the intraocular fluid. With penetrating wounds and infection, glaucoma can again de-velop secondary to swelling. Finally, injury to the eye that causes dis-placement of the lens forward (termed luxation or subluxation of the lens) causes it to press against the edge of the pupil, and this mechani-cally blocks the flow of intraocular fluid. This same luxation may occur when a cataract becomes mature and shrinks. This causes a tug on the tiny zonules that hold the lens in place. These may then rupture and the lens become free to press against the edge of the pupil.

The most dramatic changes are seen when the flow of fluid is blocked suddenly and completely. Such eyes are usually obviously bulging, with increased tearing, a whitish cast to the cornea, and obvious pain. If the obstruction is less than complete, the increase in pressure is more gradual. Such eyes may not be obviously bulging, although testing with a special instrument called a tonometer can pick up the change. The only obvious sign may be shyness around the head as the horse seeks to avoid any contact with the painful eye. Such cases of incomplete blockage are the most dangerous as they can go unnoticed while the increased pressures slowly but surely cause damage to the eye that could result in blindness in the later years.

Treatment of glaucoma involves two basic steps. The first is to remove the excess fluid and the second to treat the cause. In severe cases it is often necessary to remove the extra fluid with a small needle and syringe. This is a delicate procedure; however, it is possible to perform it with only sedation and local anesthesia to the eye. Once the immediate threat of increased intraocular pressure has been removed, the horse is treated with steroids to quickly reduce any inflammation. The steroids are usually placed directly under the thin membrane surrounding the sclera (the white of the eye) to achieve high local concentration and may also be given by injection or orally for a few additional days. With periodic ophthalmia or infectious causes, antibiotics are also commonly used, both locally as above—termed a subconjunctival injection—and systemically. Finally, drugs to facilitate the outflow of the intraocular fluid (the medical term for the intraocular fluid is aqueus humor) and relieve spasm and pain inside the eye are given by drops or subconjunctival injection. These drugs cause the pupils to constrict and may make it difficult for the horse to see in dark areas and/or at night. They are called miotics because they cause this constriction of the pupil, which is called miosis. The miotics are also used for long-term therapy of glaucoma, except in cases where the position of a luxated lens causes further blockage when the pupil is constricted.

PERIODIC OPHTHALMIA

In humans the two major causes of declining vision with damage to the back of the eye (the retina and optic nerve) are diabetes mellitus and hypertension (high blood pressure). Neither of these syndromes are a problem in horses. However, horses can suffer permanent retinal damage, together with damage to the rest of the eye, as a result of periodic ophthalmia, commonly known as "moon blindness." The name moon blindness originates from the tendency of this disease to follow a waxing and waning course, once believed to be related to the phases of the moon.

We know now that periodic ophthalmia is caused by an allergic reaction, usually to the blood-borne life stages of the parasite onchocerca or the bacteria-like organism leptospira.

The exact mechanism of the disease is unclear. It is possible that these agents have a predisposition for the tissues of the eye and attach there so that when the body mounts an antibody response against them it also attacks the tissues of the eye. Another possibility is that there are one or more proteins in the makeup of the organisms that are similar to those of the eye, making it so that the antibodies against the infection also react against the eye. In any event, both infestations are likely to have a carrier state, so that once the infestation is established the horse is continually exposed to the organism that arises from an internal focus. The body then becomes hypersensitive to the infection, and the extreme inflammatory reaction that is mounted against these organisms causes tremendous tissue damage.

During an attack, any and all levels of the eye may be affected. The cornea is usually white—the result of fluid pooling and inflammation. Blood vessels may invade the cornea as well. The deeper tissues also are inflamed, and collections of blood and white blood cells may be visible if the cornea is not completely opacified. The end result is scarring, which impairs vision with each attack and can result in blindness.

The mainstay of therapy for periodic ophthalmia is steroids. These are administered by local injection and systemically in hopes of quieting the inflammation so that permanent scarring is minimal.

To determine the cause of periodic ophthalmia, samples of fluid from within the eye can be tested for antibodies to leptospira. Blood levels of such antibodies are also measured. Although this test is not one hundred percent accurate, the presence of antibodies, particularly when the levels are highest in the fluid from the eye, strongly supports a diagnosis of leptospirosis, the disease caused by leptospira.

Onchocerciasis, the second major disease causing periodic ophthalmia, involves onchocerca, a thin worm that lives in the large ligament along the top of the neck—the ligamentum nuchae. In its adult form, it is relatively harmless. However, these adults produce tiny immature worms called microfilaria that travel throughout the body and can cause a severe allergic reaction.

Specific treatment for either disease is difficult. Once a horse becomes a carrier of leptospira it is very difficult to eliminate the infection entirely, although long-term treatment with the antibiotic dihydrostreptomycin may be tried. This requires close medical supervision as this class of antibiotics can cause damage to the kidneys and/or deafness. There is no known treatment for the elimination of the adult onchocerca worm. It is possible to kill the microfilaria with the same drug that is used in dogs to prevent heartworm disease—diethylcarbamazine (DEC). However, use of this drug in the face of a large number of the microfilaria may cause a violent reaction in the eye. Some protection is afforded by pretreating the horse with steroids and other drugs, such as antihistamines, in hopes of preventing or minimizing the reaction, but the risk remains considerable. If it is decided to try DEC, periodic retreatments will be necessary to destroy new microfilaria, or the horse may be tried on a daily dose of DEC.

BLINDNESS

When an aged horse develops a problem with vision that results in blindness, the immediate question is whether or not he should be euthanized.

There are many blind horses around that have learned to cope with their disability, and some perform almost unbelievable feats by learning to have complete trust in their riders. There is even a blind horse in England who is owned by a blind woman (and the woman makes her living by painting)! There are too many blind horses around to say it is inhumane to keep alive a horse who is blind; however, the decision to do so must be based on how well the horse copes and how committed the owner is to maintaining his safety.

Horses are very adept at learning the details of their stalls or turnout facilities, and many blind horses seem to behave just like a normal horse when in familiar surroundings. They also seem to have a heightened sense of touch and use their nose hairs to locate objects in strange places. Some even buck, play, and run when outside, stopping just short of fence lines as if they could see them.

When faced with a horse that is going blind, you must realistically evaluate several factors about that horse before taking on the task of maintaining such an animal. First, ask yourself what it was about the horse that led you to suspect he was having difficulty seeing. If it was only problems with new surroundings or reluctance to jump, the horse has probably adjusted well to the routines of life. Next, ask yourself how he reacts to changes in his familiar environment, such as moving the buckets around in his stall. If he detects the change with a minimum of effort that is good, but if he becomes obviously agitated and has trouble finding them he is not adjusting very well. Also, consider how the horse reacts to unfamiliar people or animals or simply an unfamiliar voice or sound. If he immediately becomes attentive and focuses on the strange intruder he is behaving in a normal and appropriate way, but if he panics or becomes hostile you have a potential disaster waiting to happen, and the strain of protecting him from such disturbances could be far more than you bargained for. Other factors to be considered are how well he trailers and how he reacts to sudden sounds that are likely to be a part of his daily life.

Even the horse who seems to handle the above circumstances well could fall apart if he becomes ill (e.g., colic) or injured, as even an otherwise normal horse often behaves erratically at such times. The blind horse could also be seriously hurt by a misplaced pitchfork or the development of a hole or slippery spot in his paddock. It is important that you ask yourself how you would feel if the horse were injured in some way that was related to his blindness and you did not discover the problem until the next day. Owners who know their horse well and feel he is otherwise happy with his life could accept such an accident as a fact of life, not unlike any other kind of accident to a sighted horse. However, if you were vacillating in the decision to try to maintain this horse and/or knew he was not making as good an adjustment as could be hoped, the guilt will be with you for a long time.

Such decisions are difficult indeed, and many owners wish they did not have such control over how or if a horse is to live. Deciding becomes easier, however, when you understand the details of the horse's condition and how it can affect him. It is also wise to exhaust the list of "What if..." situations, because living with a host of doubts and fears takes away the joy of even having the horse and could result in crushing remorse if something did go wrong. It is good to ask the advice of your veterinarian and anyone else you trust—but remember the final decision rightfully belongs to you. The owner who knows and loves his or her horse and understands the details of the situation will usually make the right decision.

7

The Gastrointestinal Tract

The best feed in the world will do the horse no good if it cannot be digested properly. Proper digestion requires health of the lips, teeth, oral cavity, esophagus, stomach, small intestine, and large intestine. In addition, the microorganisms that inhabit the intestinal tract must be present in the proper numbers and proportions if the horse is to derive any benefit from the many complicated carbohydrate sources he eats.

The maintenance of good digestive function in the older horse requires more than an adequate worming schedule. A malfunction of any of the digestive components will affect the others. Once this complicated system is disrupted, it can be quite difficult to restore normal function.

TUMORS OF THE LIPS AND TONGUE

To begin at the beginning, good digestion begins with the intake and chewing of food. The lips and tongue are occasionally the site of tumors in the older horse. When a tumor is detected early, surgical removal and possible implantation of radioactive materials into the tumor site can cure or control the tumor for many months or years. If undetected, the tumor size and spread to adjacent tissues may be a death sentence. Anytime a horse is exhibiting signs of difficulty chewing (dropping feed or throwing it around), a careful examination should be made for growths in the mouth.

TEETH

Far more common than tumors is a problem with the teeth. A horse's teeth are arranged so that the back teeth (molars and premolars) overlap at the sides. This leads to the development of sharp points on the buccal (cheek) side of the upper arcade and on the lingual (tongue) side of the lowers. In addition, the last teeth often develop points that hang straight down or even curve to form hooks resembling tusks. "Floating" is the process of removing these sharp points with metal files.

Floating should only be done by a professional. Once mastered, it can be done quickly, effectively, and with minimal disturbance of the horse. However, the inexperienced operator will usually find it exhausting and have trouble with restraining the horse, resulting in an incomplete job, particularly where the most distant teeth are concerned. In fact, the back teeth are missed so often that it is not unusual to find hooks that require the use of large shearers to cut and remove the growth.

Failure to float the teeth often enough leads to cuts in the mouth that make chewing painful. When feed is incompletely chewed it is very difficult to digest and you will commonly see whole kernels of grain in the manure. Other signs include dropping or throwing grain, excessive salivation when eating, and holding the head to one side. He may also resent pressure from the halter or bridle when turning. This can also lead to colic or "choke" (discussed later). Horses vary in how often they need to have their teeth floated. The average interval is once yearly, but there are a fair number that need floating every six months.

To check for points on the teeth, reach into the mouth and grab the tongue, then pull the tongue out to one side. This prevents the horse from closing his mouth and allows you to run your hand inside the cheek on the side away from the tongue to feel for points along the upper teeth. The lower teeth can be checked by hand or with a flashlight. This examination only takes seconds to perform, and there is no missing the points. Occasionally, however, the horse may be showing problems with chewing when the teeth seem to be in good shape. This could be due to hooks on the back teeth, as described earlier. To check for this, it is necessary to place your hand well inside the horses mouth. If you are unwilling, or unable, to check this area effectively, consult your veterinarian.

Other problems with the teeth that will interfere with chewing include broken or missing teeth and infections of the teeth. Broken or missing teeth are usually the result of trauma, although long-term infection of a tooth can have this end result also. Broken or missing teeth interfere with chewing by interrupting the normal dental surface. The pain of broken teeth may also cause the horse to incompletely chew his feed. A

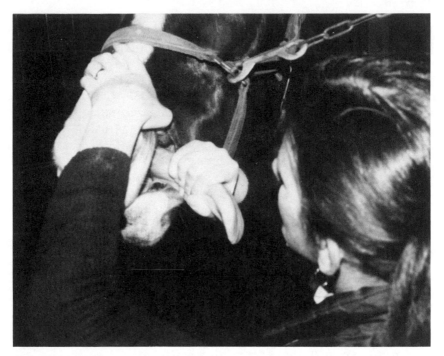

*To examine the mouth and back teeth, you must first pull out the
tongue by grasping it through the natural gap between the incisors
and check teeth.*

careful dental examination will reveal this problem, and broken teeth
should be removed as soon as possible to avoid root (and subsequent
sinus) infections.

Root Infections

While horses are not particularly prone to caries (cavities), these can
occur and cause root infections. Root infections may also result from
foreign bodies that become lodged deep in the tissues of the mouth or
through broken teeth. In addition to abnormal chewing, clinical signs
may include facial swelling over the affected area, drainage of a foul discharge from one side of the nose, and pain on palpation of the affected
area of the face. Treatment for infected teeth is surgical and requires
general anesthesia. The molars are usually involved and extraction of
these teeth is very difficult. The horse will be typed and crossed for blood
in the event of hemorrhage and will almost always be placed on antibiot-

ics before and after surgery to avoid the complications of releasing bacteria from the tooth abscess into the blood stream (possible complications being infection of joints or the heart). After surgery, there will be a hole in the horse's head where bone was removed to gain access to the tooth. This will have to be flushed once or twice daily with large amounts of water or other solution to prevent mucus, pus, and blood from building up in the sinus. Most horses strongly resist this treatment, probably more from a fear that they are in danger of drowning than from any discomfort, and even relatively strong restraint measures such as a twitch or lip chain may not be effective. (Note: One very effective method of treating horses that strongly resist is to attach a rope to the tail and clip a second one to the bottom halter ring. These ropes are then slowly passed through the bars of the stall and gently taken up until the horse is firmly against the wall. The sinus can then be flushed from outside the stall and most horses will stand quietly [it also works well for horses that are very difficult to give injections]. Furthermore, the horse does not seem to develop any aversion to having the ropes applied on subsequent treatments as long as it is always done quietly and without fuss.)

Common location for trephination (drilling a hole) to gain access to infected teeth.

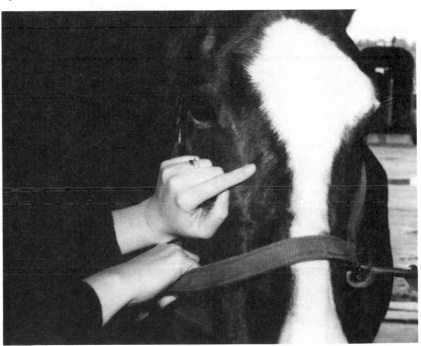

"CHOKE"

Once chewed, feed must be swallowed and transported to the stomach. These are functions we normally take for granted, but the older horse may develop problems with swallowing that eventually present as a "choke." Choke is the term used to describe food that is caught in the esophagus somewhere between the back of the throat and the stomach. The horse is not really choking as there is no food in his airway. However, he may cough and retch, leading to the term choke. Additional signs include depression, anxiety, heavy salivation from the mouth, and total refusal of food and water. These last three signs are directly related to the inability of anything to get past the obstruction in the esophagus.

It must be noted that the clinical signs just described for choke may be indistinguishable from rabies. Unless you were actually present and saw the horse take a mouthful of feed, swallow, and immediately begin to cough and retch, do not assume the problem is choke. Above all do not try to feel the back of the horse's throat for a blockage. If it is choke, the problem will be further down, and if it is not choke you will be exposing yourself unnecessarily to a risk of rabbies. Contact the veterinarian instead.

Older horses are more prone to choke. It is believed that aging is associated with a gradual degeneration of one or more of the nerves that control normal swallowing and propulsion of food down the esophagus. Another complicating factor is poor teeth that lead to improper chewing of food. A common history involves the feeding of corn on the cob, but the horse may "choke" on hay or grain also. Another common predisposing cause is an inadequate or dirty water supply and/or a lameness that makes the horse less likely to travel to his water source if he is on turnout. Similarly, the lame horse may have trouble competing for water during the winter or negotiating slippery banks to ponds or streams.

Choke is a medical emergency. Dehydration can occur rapidly and the pressure of the food on the esophagus can cause ulcers or even rupture. Once the esophagus is damaged, subsequent scarring will cause a narrowed area that is also defective in its ability to move the food along, making repeated episodes more likely.

When the blockage is detected early, before the trapped food becomes dried out and the esophagus swollen around it, it is often possible to push the blockage into the stomach with a stomach tube and the careful addition of small amounts of water and mineral oil. The main danger here is that the horse will inhale these materials and develop a severe pneumonia. Before even attempting to pass the stomach tube, the veterinarian will often administer a mild sedative and the drug atropine and place the horse in a quiet stall. This will sometimes result in the food being passed down. If not, the atropine will help to relieve any spasm of the esophagus so that the stomach tube may be used more effectively. Opinion is divided on how much sedation and/or tranquilization is advisable, as these drugs impair the horse's ability to block the passage of food and liquids into his lungs. Some veterinarians will use large doses to cause the horse to lower his head and relax the esophagus and throat, and to prevent struggling. With the horse's head lowered, the chances of material entering the lung are minimized. Others feel more comfortable with very light sedation and rely more heavily on repeated doses of atropine and keeping the horse calmly in a stall. Regardless of the approach, perseverance will often result in the stomach tube being able to push the food along.

If a choke cannot be relieved in this way, the next step is to place the horse under general anesthesia. With the horse asleep, it is possible to place a tube in the trachea that will protect the lungs and allow more aggressive use of fluids and the stomach tube. If this still fails to dislodge the blockage, surgery is the only alternative.

The actual surgery is not a difficult procedure to perform. However, the risk of scarring and later blockage, as described, is considerable and increases the longer the choke has been present. For this reason, the decision to proceed with the operation should be made very carefully and after detailed discussion with the surgeon. Also, following surgery the horse will have a hole in his neck as suturing shut the esophagus usually increases the chances that postoperative narrowing will be severe enough to cause problems. This hole will heal on its own, but you must be prepared to clean the area several times daily as food will leak out until healing is nearly complete.

COLIC

The final and major step in the digestve process involves the stomach and intestines. In a general sense, the older horse seems to be less tolerant of any changes in his feeding routine. This can be attributed in part to the accumulated damage of a lifetime of parasite exposure, although gradual deterioration in the nerve supply to the intestines is also a possibility.

The end result of this is a greater tendency for the older horse to experience nonsurgical or "spasmadic" colic. During such an episode, the intestines are in spasm in some places and very flaccid in others. This prevents the normal flow of material through the tract resulting in distention of the intestinal organs and gas development with resultant pain, dehydration, and electrolyte imbalances. A history of large strongyle ("bloodworm") infestations is very commonly associated with this problem. The colic may be triggered by a change in feed, decrease in water consumption, change in quality of the feed, unusual exercise, shipping, or anything that interferes with the horse's eating and drinking pattern. Attacks can also occur with no obvious predisposing factor, and repeated episodes are common.

Treatment involves medication to relieve the pain and spasm (usually dypyrone or Banamine), passage of a stomach tube to relieve any fluid back-up, fluids intravenously and by stomach tube to correct dehydration and electrolyte disturbances, and mineral oil to relieve any impaction that might develop and/or enemas for impaction. Prevention involves the elimination of any active contributing factors, such as parasites, and adjustments to management techniques.

When water supply is insufficient or of poor quality, or water consumption is decreased for any reason, the combination of this and reduced intestinal motility can easily result in impaction/constipation and result in abdominal pain. You can attempt to relieve this by feeding bran mashes laced with approximately a pint of mineral oil (if the horse will eat it). However, if this is not successful, veterinary attention to tube the horse with mineral oil and possibly additional fluid will be needed. Always be alert to any decrease in the amount of feces the horse is putting out so that problems such as this can be caught and treated early.

The opposite problem, diarrhea, can be quite difficult to treat in older horses. Older horses have decreased digestive efficiency, including decreased amounts of digestive enzymes and a more fragile population of bacteria and protozoa in the large intestine (where fermentation of roughages occurs). Factors such as stress, feed change, "bad feed" or an intestinal infection can initiate the diarrhea. Successful treatment/elimination of the initiating cause, however, will not necessarily resolve the diarrhea. This is usually because the intestinal population of bacteria and protozoa has been greatly altered.

An older horse with diarrhea requires veterinary attention both to diagnose and treat the cause and also to provide supplemental water and electrolytes, by stomach tube or intravenously, until the diarrhea resolves or the horse is comfortable enough to take in adequate amounts on his own. If diarrhea persists and bacterial/protozoal imbalance in the large intestines is suspected, treatment with the drug iodochlorhydroxyquin may help. Also helpful is allowing the horse to graze in pastures heavily used by other horses so that he can pick up the correct, normal microorganisms from the feces of other horses (much in the same way as foals pick up their population of normal organisms). In extreme cases, the horse may have to be tubed with fluid strained from normal feces in attempts to repopulate his intestinal tract with the beneficial organisms.

The older horse, of course, is also susceptible to any of the other causes of colic, such as parasite damage, twisted intestine, or colitis. The important thing to realize here is that the digestive tract of the older horse is already less efficient and in more precarious balance than in a younger animal. Any sign of colic/abdominal pain, including loss of appetite and depression, should be brought to the attention of the veterinarian. Early intervention is the key to avoiding life-threatening situations and hastening recovery times.

Management Techniques for Horses with Chronic Colic

Management of the horse with chronic colic involves measures to prevent the factors listed above that can precipitate an attack. Specifically, care should be taken that the amount and type of grain and hay remains relatively constant and that water is always available. Regular exercise, with rider or by turnout, is very beneficial, but unaccustomed heavy exercise should be avoided. If impaction is an associated problem, regular feedings of a mash, with or without mineral oil added, may help, and it may be advisable to have the horse tubed with mineral oil as a precautionary measure if he will be shipped or worked heavier than usual and has a history of colic and/or impaction following these activities. (This will involve a visit from the veterinarian, but experience will tell you if the cost is saving you money in the long run by decreasing the colic episodes.)

Dietary manipulations may also be indicated for the horse with chronic colic. Some horses will do best on a diet that includes large amounts of fiber and therefore liberal amounts of grass or mixed hay. Others have less difficulty when the feed quality is kept very high with appropriate amounts of straight alfalfa. The type of grain fed is usually not a problem as long as the horse is protected from drastic changes. However, crimping, rolling, or cracking of feeds will ease the burden on the digestive tract and are a good idea for the aged horse. You may find that pelleted feeds are tolerated better than grains, or vice versa. Since any manipulation of feed is likely to cause a colic attack, it is a good general rule to exhaust the other management recommendations above before trying to change the diet. If these do not give satisfactory results, experimenting with the diet may be started, but with care taken to make changes very gradually. Substitutions should be made at a rate of 10 percent of the total ration per day, giving complete switch-over in ten days, and you should stop at any given level (or even reverse to the previous level of substitution) if the horse shows discomfort. Such setbacks do not necessarily mean that you are on the wrong track and could be due to a totally unrelated problem. You can resume the substitution process after the horse has been normal for two days, possibly taking even more time by switching at 5 percent per day. Any horse who colics on a schedule this conservative should be switched back to the original feed.

All older horses, and particularly those with a history of colic or other digestive problems, need a carefully planned and faithfully followed worming schedule. This is discussed in detail in the chapters on routine health care and turnout (Chapters 2 and 15). The reason for these precautions is that the horse gradually loses his ability to fight off parasite infestations as he ages, and he becomes susceptible to both a wider range of parasites and to higher parasite burdens. Unless your horse is kept under experimental conditions, it is never safe to assume that he has no parasites. These life forms have so many complicated and effective ways to maintain their existence that all horses have some level of parasitism, and any foothold is likely to escalate into a significant problem for the aged horse.

Enteroliths

Another cause of colic that is more likely in aged horses is enterolith formation. An enterolith is a large, rock-hard mass found inside the intestine. The outer layer is very firmly packed minerals. The core contains some piece of indigestible foreign material that the horse ate years before. Common offenders are pieces of rubber or baling twine. Since these objects cannot be digested, they will lie in the intestine and gradually collect a layer of feces that is very dense and dry. Enteroliths vary in size from one to five pounds or more. The first sign of trouble may be only a vague abdominal discomfort with no obvious abnormalities, even on rectal examination. In time, however, enteroliths become large enough to block the intestine and must be surgically removed. The risks and complications of surgery are very much the same as for any abdominal procedure and include adverse reactions to the anesthetic, infection of the abdominal cavity, formation of scar tissues (adhesions) between sections of the bowel (which will cause pain later), and the risk of injury during the recovery period. However, horses with enteroliths are usually in better condition before surgery than those with conditions that involve actual damage to or destruction of a segment of the intestines (e.g., "twisted" intestines) and therefore have a better overall chance of surviving the immediate intraoperative and postoperative periods. The surgeon can help you to understand the details and pros and cons of an abdominal procedure and what to expect after surgery. Always feel free to ask questions until you are satisfied you have enough information to make an informed decision.

ABDOMINAL ABSCESSES

Older horses are also more likely to develop problems related to abdominal abscesses. The abscess may be located along the intestine itself, on the abdominal wall, or in some other abdominal organ. These infections are usually the result of severe infections that the horse experienced before the age of two that have long since been forgotten. They may also form at the site of a previous surgery or wound. Abscesses contain bacteria that the body has surrounded with a heavy coating of scar tissue to seal them off. A horse and his abscess can coexist for many, many years with absolutely no sign that there is a problem. However, in sealing the organisms away from the body the horse has also prevented the blood and infection-fighting cells from gaining access to the bacteria, and as a result the abscess will grow very slowly but steadily over time. Abscesses become a problem when they become large enough to interfere with the intestines by pressing on them and/or when their size actually causes signs of abdominal pain when the horse moves. It is not unusual for an abdominal abscess to be the size of a cantaloupe before it is discovered, and they have been reported to weigh twenty pounds or more.

Diagnosis is made by blood tests that may uncover evidence of a process of chronic inflammation and/or infection and by rectal examination. Some abscesses, however, defy detection because their weight carries them to the bottom of the abdomen and out of the reach of the veterinarian while the slow growth pattern causes little change in the blood picture. These are usually diagnosed only at the time of surgery.

There are two approaches to therapy: long-term antibiotic administration and surgery. When clinical signs are relatively mild (low-grade colic, low or no fever), antibiotics can be tried in hopes of getting enough inside the abscess to cause it to shrink and to kill the bacteria. This is a very slow process due to the poor blood supply and will require several months of therapy. But since it does not take long for a horse to tire of intramuscular injections, administration of antibiotics may be a problem. However, there are a few antibiotics that can be given in the feed and are well tolerated for long periods of time. Complete success rates are less than one hundred percent with this approach, but it is often possible to control the abscess to the point that clinical signs disappear.

When the abscess is causing obvious problems with colic, fever, and abdominal pain, surgery may be the only course available. If at all possible, a course of antibiotics prior to surgery is indicated, for several days to several weeks depending upon the severity of the clinical signs and the need for immediate surgical intervention. The success rate with surgery will be directly dependent upon where the abscess is located, which organs and other structures are involved in the abscess, and the size of the mass. Complications include rupture of the abscess with massive infection of the abdomen as a result. This is cause for immediate euthanasia as even if the infection could be controlled, the scarring in the abdomen as a result of this type of contamination would interfere with intestinal function and cause chronic pain. This and other possible complications of surgery should be discussed at length with the surgeon before deciding whether to proceed. It will probably be impossible for him to give you any detailed percentage rates for success until all the facts are uncovered at surgery, but your horse's general chances and the common complications (short- and long-term) of abdominal surgery can be detailed.

ABDOMINAL TUMORS

Finally, increasing age carries a rising frequency of tumors involving the abdomen. Cancers arising directly from the bowel or other organs are very rare. However, the horse does sometimes develop growths called lipomas that originate in the fat tissue. These are not cancerous but can cause problems as they are frequently located at the end of a long, slender stalk that may become wrapped around a piece of intestine and cause strangulation of blood supply and obstruction to the flow of intestinal contents. The abdomen may also be the site of widespread cancers such as lymphosarcoma. Melanomas that originate around the anus can also eventually spread to the abdomen. Clinical signs are those related to cancer in general (debilitation, weight loss) as well as fluid collection in the abdomen (ascites) and possible problems from large growths impinging on blood supply, nerves, or the intestinal tract (see Chapter 12, "Tumors," for more details).

ADVANCES IN ABDOMINAL SURGERY

Abdominal problems serious enough to require surgical correction were often a death sentence to the older horse. The combined stresses of surgery, anesthesia, blood loss, prolonged periods in abnormal positions during surgery, complications of infection, and others are frequently too much for the older horse to tolerate. Recent advances in equine surgery may change this dramatically for some horses.

Equine surgery has moved into the era of laparoscopic surgery. In this technique, an endoscope (much like the one used to examine the upper airways, throat, and bronchial tree of the lungs) is passed into the abdomen through a very small "stab" incision. This allows the surgeon to determine exactly what the nature of the problem is and to plan the necessary procedure. This alone saves valuable time under anesthesia and prevents unnecessary surgery in cases that can be managed medically or are so severe that the prognosis for correction and survival with surgery is too low to warrant operating.

Of even greater advantage is the possibility that the surgery can be done laparoscopically. The surgeon uses the laparoscope to see what is going on and makes one or more additional, small "stab" incisions to allow the insertion of special instruments or laser equipment to actually perform the procedure.

In this way, many problems that would otherwise have required a large incision, more extensive blood loss and a prolonged and stressful recovery period can be accomplished with much less stress to the horse. For example, a horse with a lipoma (fatty tumor) can develop problems when the long stalk of the tumor becomes wrapped around a section of the intestine. Using laparoscopic technique, the stalk of the tumor can be cut and all the bleeding stopped without a major incision. The tumor could then be brought up against the body wall and an incision made to extract it without ever handling and potentially damaging the other contents of the abdomen. The bowel itself can even be cut, a section removed and the ends sewn back together without entering the abdomen with anything more than the laparoscope and the laparoscopic instruments.

The end result is a much lower risk of major complications such as hemorrhage, infection, or the formation of adhesions (intra-abdominal scars that may require another surgery in the future). The anesthesia time required is much less as well. The horse thus recovers much more quickly and with fewer problems, reducing time in the hospital and increasing the likelihood he will return to a normal life.

Aging is associated with a number of processes that affect digestion. However, most can be prevented or controlled by careful attention to proper management, feeding, and worming practices. If trouble does develop, timely attention from the veterinarian is indicated to avoid severe upset of the intestinal microorganisms and/or the bodywide effects of dehydration and electrolyte imbalance.

8

The Cardiovascular System

hen compared to many other animal species, particularly hu mans, the horse has a relatively low incidence of serious heart problems. Complicating this picture, however, could be an ignorance of many of the cardiac problems of old age as most horses are either euthanized before they become old enough to develop such troubles or are never autopsied or followed by regular medical examinations. About all that can be stated is that very few horses are ever brought to the attention of the veterinarian for complaints that are obviously cardiac in nature.

Nevertheless, there are several syndromes of cardiac disease that are associated with aging. These include disease of the blood vessels, heart valves, and heart rhythm. One problem we do not see with any frequency is the familiar "heart attack," which is caused by plugging of one or more of the arteries that feed the heart itself, resulting in severe damage or destruction of heart muscle and abnormal cardiac function. (Perhaps in part due to the fact that horses do not smoke, eat high-fat diets, or fail to exercise regularly!)

SUDDEN DEATH

There is no one particular syndrome of cardiac disease that stands out as most common. The most dramatic, however, is sudden death caused by rupture of the heart muscle or one of the great vessels of the heart (an

Figure 8. Top View of Heart and Major Vessels

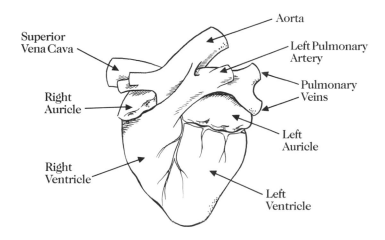

Aorta

Superior Vena Cava

Left Pulmonary Artery

Pulmonary Veins

Right Auricle

Left Auricle

Right Ventricle

Left Ventricle

aorta or pulmonary artery). The usual history is that the horse simply collapsed and died during some stressful activity such as breeding or exercise. In other cases the horse may be found dead with the exact circumstances surrounding his demise unclear.

Such ruptures may occur at the site of an aneurysm, which is a dilated area with weakened walls that develops in time in an area that is subjected to high blood pressures throughout life. Such areas include the left side of the heart, the aorta, and any of the large vessels entering or leaving the heart (see Figure 8). A history of chronic lung disease can be associated with elevated pressures in the pulmonary artery and the right side of the heart, which make this side of the cardiovascular system more prone to rupture.

Sudden death of cardiac origin is usually not associated with any warning signs, and the horse may have appeared to be perfectly normal up to the time of death. In any event, there is no definitive treatment to be tried as open-chest or large-vessel surgery are not viable options in horses since their large size makes simply getting to these areas technically difficult and at this time we do not have the technology available to support a horse (i.e., heart and lung machines). However, early and aggressive treatment of respiratory disease can minimize the chances of right-sided heart stress. The most important fact to remember is that this sudden death syndrome becomes more likely with age. Therefore the older horse should be protected from unaccustomed exercise or excitement as much as possible.

Figure 9. Cross Section of Heart Showing Valves and Septae

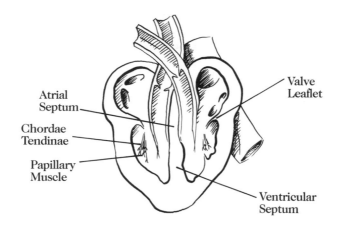

Atrial Septum

Chordae Tendinae

Papillary Muscle

Valve Leaflet

Ventricular Septum

VALVULAR DISEASE

Disease of the heart valves also becomes more likely with age, with the aortic valve the most likely to be involved in the horse. The changes of valvular disease include thickening of the valve edges and/or disease of the tiny muscles that control their movement—the chordae tendinae (see Figure 9). The result is a valve that does not open and close normally and thus interferes with proper filling and emptying of blood in the heart. This in turn raises pressures within the heart and causes the heart to work harder, which can lead to heart failure.

Heart failure is characterized by shortness of breath, decreased exercise tolerance, and fluid accumulation in the lungs, legs, or abdomen. However, clinical evidence of heart failure is not often seen in horses. Part of the reason for this is the relative rarity of valvular disease in the first place, coupled with the horse's inherently very efficient cardiovascular system and athletically active lifestyle that give him quite a bit of reserve to draw from even when the heart is compromised. In addition, the decreased demands made on an old horse make him less likely to exceed his heart's capacity and develop heart failure.

Bacterial Endocarditis

In addition to the nonspecific valvular changes described earlier, a horse may suffer from bacterial endocarditis, which is infection of the edges of the heart valves with colonies of bacteria. Bacterial endocarditis may follow a severe infection anywhere on the body and is most likely when there are high fevers indicating that the bacteria are actually circulating in the blood and not limited to a local infection site such as a wound. Bacterial endocarditis results in the growth of small nodules called vegetations on the edges of the heart valves. These interfere with normal valve opening and closing and can lead to the same problems as described earlier. In addition, bacterial endocarditis often causes periods of unexplained fever and a chronic debilitated state with weight loss and weakness secondary to repeated releases of bacteria from vegetations into the blood.

Heart Murmurs

Diagnosis of valvular disease is made by listening to (ausculting) the heart and hearing an abnormal murmur. Murmurs are caused by abnormal pressures and flows of blood across the valves and also by valves that fail to open and close normally. It can be very difficult to ascertain the significance of a murmur heard in a horse as the large size of his heart, the large flows of blood, and the wide variations in how the heart is positioned inside the chest can all cause a variety of murmurs that are perfectly "normal," since a murmur is just a sound made by blood flowing through the heart that tells you nothing about precisely what is causing the sound.

For example, I acquired my first horse because a grade V murmur (the worst grade) was detected when he was being vetted for sale as a very expensive open-jumper prospect. Extensive studies were done to determine what was causing the murmur, but no pathology could be found. Strangest of all was that the murmur actually disappeared as the horse was worked hard. I had the horse well into his teens and he never showed any signs of exercise intolerance. In fact, he had tremendous speed and loved to show it every opportunity he got! After he was finally euthanized (for a lameness), an autopsy revealed that his heart was totally normal structurally--but the largest that anyone could ever remember seeing. The final theory was that his great heart simply pumped such large flows that the resulting sounds were outside the range of "normal."

Although this case was very interesting, in most cases murmurs above a grade III on a scale of I to V are indicative of pathology. Further details of the horse's condition can be obtained from an electrocardiogram, catheterization of the heart, or by echocardiography.

Electrocardiograms also show a wide variation in normal due to the vast differences among horses in heart size, chest size, and heart positioning. An experienced cardiologist, however, can pick up abnormalities that indicate strain or abnormal rhythms. In cardiac catheterization, a small tube is introduced into the heart to measure pressures. This procedure can be done with relative ease for the right side of the heart by entering the jugular vein in the neck. Abnormal pressures here indicate disease of the valves or muscle on the right side or problems with circulation through the lungs. To obtain left-sided pressures, it is necessary to enter a major artery, and this requires that the horse be heavily sedated or under general anesthesia. The risks are higher and the data is less reliable because of the need for anesthesia. For these reasons left-sided catheterization is rarely done. Finally, echocardiography is a technique where sound waves are bounced off the chest and form a picture on an oscilloscope screen. The image corresponds to the walls and valves, and it is often possible to detect gross abnormalities with this technique.

Heart murmurs may also be caused by holes in the wall between the two sides of the heart. These are called septal defects, interatrial for between the upper chambers or atria and interventricular for between the ventricles or lower chambers. These defects are present at birth and are caused by a failure of the wall to completely form in the fetus. The murmurs produced are typically very loud, but their intensity rarely corresponds to the degree of compromise. In fact, many horses with murmurs of septal defects are actually racing.

Because it is rare to find a horse who is experiencing difficulties directly related to a valvular or structural problem in the heart, most cases are not given extensive diagnostic work-ups. In fact, no treatments are given unless the horse is sick with bacterial endocarditis or has chronic lung disease complicating some right-side heart problem. However, the presence of a cardiac abnormality in a horse with advancing age dictates that overly strenuous exercise be avoided. If the horse has a very active lifestyle and/or any signs of decreasing exercise tolerance, evaluation by electrocardiogram and right-sided catheterization may be recommended to establish his baseline status and to help in evaluation at intervals following the initial diagnosis. More specific recommendations regarding exercise may then be given. Echocardiograms, when available, can be helpful in pinpointing the cause of the problem.

ATRIAL FIBRILLATION

Finally, horses are more susceptible than other, smaller animals to the cardiac arrhythmia termed atrial fibrillation. With this disorder, the upper chambers of the heart beat independently of the lower chambers instead of in the normal one-to-one ratio of atrial contraction to ventricular contraction. Such horses have an irregular pulse with periods of rapid rhythm interspersed with pauses.

This disjointed contract pattern decreases the ability of the heart to effectively pump blood and does affect exercise tolerance. However, this is rarely apparent unless the animal is performing maximally, e.g., racing. The clinical presentation is usually of a nondescript poor performance rather than any dramatic signs such as loss of consciousness. The horse may also show a tendency to stop suddenly or slow down without warning.

Atrial fibrillation becomes more likely with advancing age. The cause of this is unknown, although it is possible that aging results in the inevitable loss of some of the fibers within the heart that control normal conduction of the impulses regulating contraction, and this loss tips the already delicate balance in favor of the abnormal rhythm. Fortunately, most horses can be converted to a normal rhythm with the drug quinidine and once converted usually remain in normal rhythm (suggesting there are factors at work here researchers have yet to understand). Conversion is done by giving gradually increasing doses of quinidine over several hours. Most horses can be converted over one day's treatment; however, since side effects can occur this therapy should be done in a hospital setting. Even a horse who has trouble tolerating quinidine without side effects can often be converted by resuming the drug the next day and making the increases more gradual.

Once converted, a horse needs no further treatment. However, he should be followed at regular intervals to guarantee he does not return to the abnormal rhythm. This is particularly important in the older horse, who is more likely to have an overall decrease in the efficiency of his cardiovascular system and be more intolerant of any insult. As an owner, you can help in the monitoring by learning your horse's normal resting pulse rate and making a habit of checking the pulse daily.

The normal resting pulse of a horse is between the high twenties and mid-to-high forties. Lower rates are found in horses that are very fit, while any excitement can cause a rapid (although transient) increase. The pulse can be taken by placing your fingers lightly across one of the superficial arteries, such as along the jaw or behind the fetlock (see photos on pages 110-11). Alternately, you can obtain the heart rate by placing your hand under the left elbow. The horses heart is close to the surface here and generally the beating can be easily felt.

With atrial fibrillation, the pulse will be erratic and usually will show pauses interspersed with periods of a rapid rate. This is not specific to atrial fibrillation per se but does indicate that an arrhythmia (abnormal rhythm) is present. Anytime the heart beat is irregular, a pulse deficit may be found. A pulse deficit is a discrepancy between the number of times per minute the heart is beating and how many pulses you can feel at a peripheral artery. When there is a pulse deficit, the pulse rate is less than the heart rate because some of the contractions are too disorga-

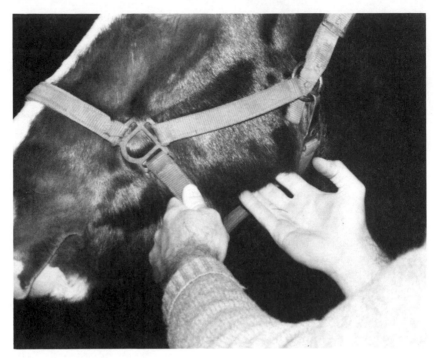

1

Three techniques for taking the pulse.

1. *Place your fingers lightly along the edge of the jaw bone, about midway between the throatlatch and the start of the cheek muscle.*
2. *Slide your hand forward under the left elbow and feel the heart beating. (This actually gives a heart rate, not a pulse, and can be compared to the pulse to see if the horse is "dropping" beats.)*
3. *Gently cup the back of the fetlock joint with your fingertips resting lightly along the middle of the inside sesamoid bone. A complex of artery, vein, and nerve runs over the top of each sesamoid, just under the skin.*

2

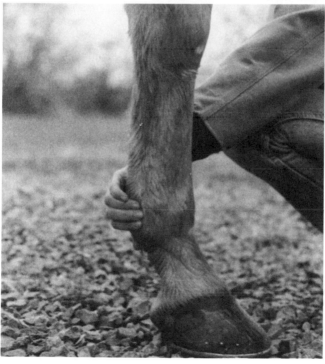

3

nized to effectively pump blood. A pulse deficit should always be brought to the attention of your veterinarian.

PRECAUTIONS

As a final note on cardiac disease, special care is indicated when the aged horse has a viral infection. Electrocardiograms taken during a viral illness sometimes reveal evidence that the myocardial muscle is directly involved in the infection. This nonspecific inflammation has not been associated with any particular problems other than the electrocardiographic abnormalities, but there is too little information on this phenomenon to write it off as harmless. There is also data to suggest that these electrocardiographic changes persist beyond the period when the horse is obviously ill with fever or depression. Since the older horse is more likely to have any of the above cardiovascular lesions as well, it is wise to allow the horse a full seven to ten days of rest following a viral infection before resuming any regular activities. This should be seven to ten days after obvious evidence of infection is gone. Stall rest is indicated when the horse is ill, but he may be turned out in a small paddock after this time. As with many other aspects of managing the older horse, the best course is always to be overcautious.

The process of aging is accompanied by an inevitable deterioration of the flexibility of the cardiovascular system. The walls of blood vessels weaken, lose their elasticity, and generally show the scars of a long life. For all of this, the horse is remarkably free of dramatic problems related to his heart, and the types of cardiac disease so common in people are almost unheard of in the horse. While older horses can therefore seem to have perfectly normal cardiovascular systems, they are more susceptible to any unusual stresses. Any signs of decreased exercise tolerance should be evaluated by your veterinarian to determine if there is a cardiovascular component that requires modification in the exercise load. Unaccustomed exercise or excitement may be poorly tolerated or could even cause sudden death. Treating the older horse like an invalid is certainly not desirable for the animal or the owner; however, a sane approach to work and a "better safe than sorry" attitude should prevail.

9

The Respiratory System

Proper functioning of the respiratory system is critical for all aged horses, whether retired to pasture or actively performing. The passage of time is accompanied by inevitable changes in how the horse responds to respiratory infections and by worsening of any pulmonary pathology.

Aging results in a decreased efficiency of the immune system—the body's capacity to fight off infections. Among the most visible consequences of this aging change is an increase in the frequency and severity of respiratory infections. The details of the respiratory viruses that infect horses, along with recommended vaccination schedules, have been presented in Chapter 2, "Routine Health Care." Vaccination—a wise investment for horses of any age—warrants particular attention for the older horse as he is more susceptible and also more likely to develop a severe disease. The complications of viral respiratory disease include the development of a bacterial infection on top of the original viral one and a worsening of any chronic respiratory condition the horse may have.

CHRONIC RESPIRATORY DISEASE

The most well-known chronic respiratory disease of the horse is "heaves." Many people use the terms heaves, emphysema, broken wind, and bronchitis interchangeably; however, all have different meanings and significance.

The term heaves comes from observation of a breathing pattern characterized by use of the abdominal muscles at the end of expiration in an effort to force air out of the lungs. The horse is heaving (laboring), and it is possible to see his belly sink in just below and behind the ribs with each breath (a "heave line"). The term heaving is very useful descriptively but really tells you very little about what exactly is going on in the lung. The heaving pattern can be seen in a horse with an acute and severe allergic or irritative reaction or in one with long-standing and permanent structural damage in his lungs. It is vital to the treatment and prognosis to get a more detailed diagnosis.

The lung reacts to a large number of allergens and irritants in a predictable manner. Mucus production increases and the small airways constrict in a sort of reflex reaction to prevent the offending agent from gaining access. Unfortunately, these reactions also prevent the entry of air, and the horse is forced to fight against his own body's defense system just to obtain enough oxygen. The substances that can cause this reaction include many dusts, pollens, molds, and even foods, as well as nonspecific irritants such as smoke, air pollution, and ammonia or other gases formed from the breakdown of urine and manure. How drastically the horse reacts is in part determined by his individual predisposition to develop allergies and in part to how directly irritating the substance is to the lung tissues. For example, any horse would have trouble breathing in a dusty riding arena, but not all would react violently to microscopic amounts of mold in the hay. Another factor that contributes to the development of bronchoconstriction (closing down of the airways) is

Location of the "heave line."

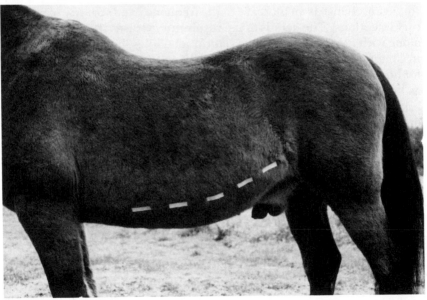

infection, with many horses having their first attack following a period of viral respiratory disease.

An acute heaves attack is very similar to asthma in humans. The predominant finding on a physical examination with auscultation of the lungs (listening with a stethoscope) is wheezing during expiration. The wheezing noise is caused by air being forced through narrowed airways. Respiratory rates are invariably increased, with the degree of heaving directly related to how severe the bronchoconstriction is.

The horse in the midst of an acute heaves attack is certainly a dramatic sight and leaves no doubt that he has considerable distress. However, the heaving is a temporary problem and will quiet down when he is removed from whatever is triggering the reaction and the inflammation and swelling in the lung have had a chance to resolve. The most common treatment is to administer the drug atropine to relieve the spasm and follow this with a course of steroids to fight inflammation. Also central to successful treatment is to attempt to isolate the offending agent by an inspection of the premises and possibly with skin tests. It is usually recommended that the horse be kept outdoors as the majority of irritants are found in the barn and/or concentrated in the air inside the barn. A complete change in feed may also be recommended. Once the attack has subsided, the horse can be re-exposed to his previous feeds and other components of the barn environment in hopes of pinpointing the source.

The acute attack will usually show prompt and dramatic response to the above measures with the horse returning to a normal respiratory rate and pattern very quickly. However, when treatment is inadequate or delayed, or if attempts to remove the horse from the source of the irritant are not successful, complications may occur. One complication is an increased susceptibility to infection—always a concern but of even more importance in an aged horse. Another even more serious complication is the development of permanent lung damage.

When the lung is forced to fight for air over prolonged periods of time, the walls of the bronchi become scarred and narrowed secondary to the inflammation. The lower areas of the lung (see Figure 10), where the alveoli are located, then develop the most serious change—emphysema.

In a normal lung, exchange of gases occurs across the alveoli. These are small sacs located at the end of the tiniest airways. The appearance of the alveoli has been likened to a cluster of grapes. The arrangement of the membrane for gas diffusion in this manner allows for the maximum surface area for contact with the air. That is, if you were to straighten out all the alveolar walls in any given area into a flat area, it would measure far larger than the circumference of the area that contains them.

With repeated, prolonged, or improperly treated heaves, the increased

Figure 10. Normal Anatomy and Advanced Chronic Lung Disease

Mainstem Bronchus

Segmental Bronchus

Terminal Bronchus

Alveoli

Bronchioles

Thickened Bronchial Walls

Emphysema

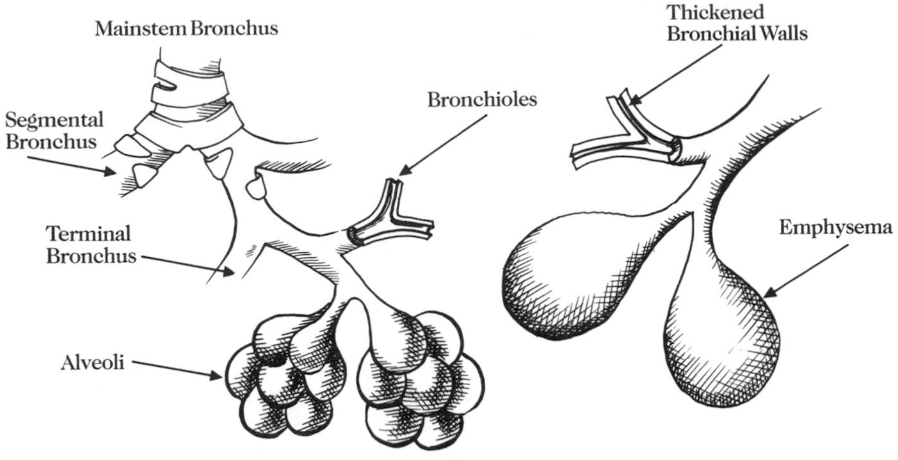

10 a.

Normal

10 b.

Advanced Chronic Lung Disease

pressures within the lung eventually cause rupture of the alveolar walls so that what once looked like a cluster of grapes may eventually look like an empty ball. This loss of surface area greatly reduces the amount of oxygen the body can absorb and also decreases the amount of carbon dioxide gas and other wastes that can be easily removed from the body and eliminated in the expired air. The eventual result is a permanently abnormal respiratory pattern with increased respiratory rates as the horse struggles to compensate for his damaged lung. No amount of drugs can restore normal breathing to such a structurally altered lung.

Exercising a Heavey Horse

In the early stages, the horse's exercise tolerance will only be decreased during an acute attack. Atropine is so successful at this stage that most horses could perform any activity within seconds of an injection. However, the effect of atropine is relatively short-lived, and it is important to allow sufficient time for the steroids to quiet any inflammation before resuming work (usually around two to three days).

With repeated attacks, the bronchial walls begin to show permanent thickening and narrowing. Such a horse may be perfectly normal at rest and with slow work but will begin to show some intolerance for prolonged or fast work, particularly when there are any complicating factors such as very cold air, high humidity, or a high level of air pollution. Working such a horse under those conditions causes the same changes in the lungs as another attack of heaves would, because work too causes breathing under high pressures within the lung. While the changes these horses have are irreversible, it is possible in a large number of cases to manage the horse in such a way that he continues to be useful.

The first step in such management is to exhaust every possibility in pinpointing the cause (hay, dust, mold) and eliminating exposure, even if it means keeping the horse outdoors year round. Step two is constant vigilance to detect any signs of worsening breathing and treating this aggressively to minimize the chances of increased damage. Third, you must make a realistic appraisal of the horse's exercise limitations and be constantly alert to changes in the weather that will require even more reduction in work. If these measures are followed faithfully, there is no reason why the horse cannot live out his natural lifespan and continue to be active. (Note: Another key element in managing such horses is the prevention of respiratory infections that compromise breathing and can trigger another heaves attack. This involves a maximum schedule of vaccination and avoidance of activities that would expose the horse to such infections, such as indoor shows.)

Emphysema

In the final stage of heaves, emphysema, the horse will probably have some problem with breathing even at rest. It is often difficult to know what to do with such horses; they are a constant care problem. Nevertheless, if the owner is willing to make the investment in time and money, many can be kept comfortable with medications, such as administration of steroids in the feed every other day. This is an acceptable approach from the viewpoint of the horse's quality of life but only for as long as he remains able to function on a daily basis and as long as the owner remains committed to providing any special environment and management he needs and to monitoring the horse closely to detect any deterioration. As with any chronically ill horse, it is important to establish guidelines for what is and what is not a humane way to continue on with the horse. On a lighter note, if the problem is detected early and treated properly with appropriate medications and management, the chances are good that the horse will never deteriorate to this point.

As previously noted, the therapy for heaves primarily involves the use of steroids. Steroids are extremely potent anti-inflammatory drugs but also affect other body systems and must always be used under the direct supervision of a veterinarian. Possible side effects include weight gain, fluid retention, electrolyte and blood-sugar abnormalities, serious infections, and founder. Other drugs that may be used include bronchodilators and/or atropine, antihistamines, and antibiotics, the latter used for short periods of time during periods that require high doses of steroids. There are a number of preparations that are marketed for addition to the feed of heavey horses. These will usually contain an antihistamine and/or the expectorant sodium iodide. While using these is not harmful, it is important for the owner to realize that relying solely upon such preparations could lead to a delay in control of inflammation, which in turn raises the risk of permanent damage.

Bleeding from the Lung

Other chronic diseases of the lung include bleeding from the lung and chronic infection and/or abscessation. Bleeding from the lung is a very common phenomenon among horses that exercise at maximal levels— i.e., racing. In fact, research on racetracks has shown that 60 percent of horses who make it into the winner's circle will reveal signs of bleeding into the lung when examined with an endoscope (a flexible instrument passed through the nostril and used to view the pharynx and deep parts of the respiratory system). Bleeding into the lung is usually only a problem for horses enduring extreme exercise, and a history of this under such circumstances does not necessarily mean the horse will have any long-term problems as a result. However, any horse who bleeds (as detected by blood trickling from the nose after exercise) with submaximal exercise should be evaluated for blood-clotting disorders and/or deep infection in the lung.

CHRONIC INFECTIONS

Chronic infection in the lung tissues is probably a far greater problem than is generally recognized and may account at least in part for horses that show a deterioration in respiratory function and exercise tolerance that is difficult to control with the usual approach to chronic respiratory disease (i.e., steroids) and for horses that are difficult to maintain in good flesh as they age. Such infections may be a low-grade chronic colonization of the respiratory tract with a bacteria or fungus or could be a deep abscess. Horses with these conditions would be nondescript "poor doers" with periods of lethargy and decreased appetite, often with low-grade fevers during such times and elevated white blood cell counts in the blood. Abscesses in the lung are a common cause of lung bleeding but could be present with no such clues if the horse were not being asked to exercise maximally. These abscesses are usually the legacy of a bacterial infection acquired as a foal that the body successfully walled off. The horse can manage quite well with this problem in his younger adult years, but the declining immune system that accompanies aging results in more significant consequences. Abscesses here (or elsewhere in the body) weaken from time to time, commonly as a result of some other insult to the tissue such as an allergy or a viral infection, and release bacteria into the lung and bloodstream at such times. This causes the periodic loss of appetite, depression, and low-grade fever. If large numbers of bacteria are released, the horse may become seriously ill with high fevers, blood, and pus draining from the lung, and systemic consequences such as founder. Another possible consequence of abscessation in the lung is the eventual erosion of the abscess into surrounding blood vessels, which causes weakening of their walls and hemorrhage that may be life-threatening, depending on the size of the vessel.

Detection of chronic lung infections is often difficult, particularly if the horse does not show any really dramatic clinical signs. The history of "doing poorly," as noted is often the only clue. The addition of even mild signs of respiratory difficulty focuses more attention to the respiratory tract, although medical attention, and hence diagnosis, is usually not sought until there are more serious indicators of disease, such as hemorrhage or high fever. Auscultation of the chest may detect areas where breath sounds are decreased. Percussion (tapping the chest) uncovers an area of dullness where the abscess is located. Definitive diagnosis requires a tracheal wash.

Tracheal washing is a technique for obtaining material from deep within the lung to be used for culture and other studies. It is done by clipping and sterilizing an area over the trachea (windpipe), making a small incision with a scalpel, and then placing a large needle into the trachea. Plastic tubing is then passed through the needle and down into the lung. Sterile fluid is injected through the tubing and then quickly pulled back. The fluid will then contain cells, mucus, and bacterial samples. The samples are then cultured and examined under a microscope for signs of bleeding, infection, or inflammation in the lung.

The treatment of chronic lung infections is often very difficult. The bacteria in such cases are usually very well established, and their control requires high doses of antibiotics over prolonged periods of time, particularly if they are "protected" within the walls of an abscess. (The walls of an abscess contain very little blood supply. This protects the body from the offending material inside but also means that drugs in the bloodstream are not delivered to the interior of the abscess very effectively.) Fungal infections are also very difficult to treat and require very potent and potentially dangerous drugs. However, despite these limitations, it is usually possible to devise an approach to the therapy of deep-seated lung infections that satisfied the criteria of effectiveness, safety, and ease of administration—as well as the owner's pocketbook.

"ROARING"

In addition to the diseases of the lung discussed already, the older horse is also more likely to suffer compromise as a result of problems in the upper airways. The most common such syndrome is "roaring."

Roaring refers to the loud noise made by a horse who has one or both vocal cords paralyzed. In a normal horse, the vocal cords are pulled out of the way when the horse breaths in. In a roarer, however, the paralyzed vocal cord hangs limply and blocks the flow of air into the lungs.

This condition is caused by disease of the recurrent laryngeal nerve, which is responsible for normal movement of the vocal cords. The left side is usually affected as the nerve on this side is very long. The length of the nerve is significant as nerve tissue must receive all its nutrition from a single cell located at its origin, and the efficiency with which the distant ends of the nerve are maintained is directly related to the length of the nerve. Also, the left recurrent laryngeal nerve loops around the aorta before traveling back up the neck to the vocal cord, and it is believed by some that the pressure from the pulse in the aorta may cause some damage to the nerve over time.

In the early stages of this disease, the horse may only make a noise when he is working very hard and may show no signs of actually having a decreased exercise tolerance despite the obvious noise. As the paralysis progresses, the noise occurs with less work and the horse may begin to show signs of decreased tolerance for work such as labored breathing and decreased ability to perform at speed.

Diagnosis is made by examination of the back of the throat with an endoscope passed through the nose (see Figure 11). An experienced veterinarian (who has small-enough hands!) can also become proficient at detecting roarers by palpating the muscles of the larynx and feeling a loss of muscle size on the paralyzed side.

The only treatment for roaring is surgical. Before recommending this, however, the veterinarian will want to know if there are any signs that the horse is having trouble performing. If he is still functioning well, even in the face of an obvious noise, it will usually be recommended that nothing be done until he is no longer able to do the work that is desired.

When surgery is recommended, there are two main types. The first and oldest approach involves removing a small sac located in the area of the vocal cord. This procedure is called a ventriculectomy. The goal is to create enough irritation and/or inflammation in the area that the scar tissues resulting from the insult of surgery will cause the vocal cord to heal in a position that is out of the airway. Success rates with ventriculectomy are approximately 60 percent. Among the advantages are that it can be done with the horse standing and under local anesthe-

Figure 11

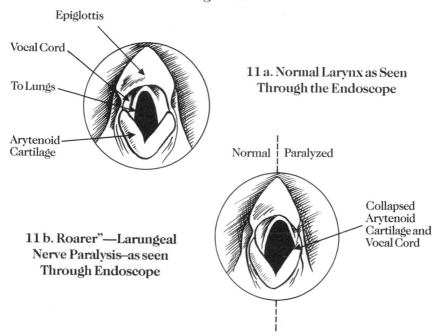

Epiglottis

Vocal Cord

To Lungs

Arytenoid Cartilage

11 a. Normal Larynx as Seen Through the Endoscope

Normal | Paralyzed

Collapsed Arytenoid Cartilage and Vocal Cord

11 b. Roarer"—Larungeal Nerve Paralysis–as seen Through Endoscope

Palpation of the larynx ("voice box") to check for muscle loss that accompanies "roaring."

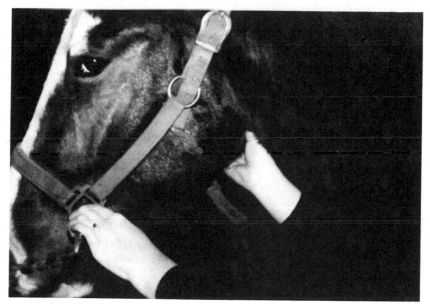

sia, thus reducing costs and eliminating the risks associated with more complicated procedures and general anesthesia.

The other procedure involves the placement of a heavy suture material that duplicates the pull of the normal laryngeal muscles and aims to anchor the vocal cord permanently out of the airway. This procedure is termed laryngeal prosthesis. It is more complicated than ventriculectomy and does require that the horse be placed under general anesthesia. Although this procedure is more expensive than the simple ventriculectomy, success rates are generally better, with an average probably being around 75 percent with good to excellent results and 80 to 90 percent with improvement.

The decision to perform surgery for this or any other condition must be made very carefully in the case of the older horse. When an animal has served a long and productive life he deserves to have the procedure viewed in terms of whether or not it is likely to benefit the quality of his life rather than just the desires of the owner. Some of the risks of anesthesia, such as cardiovascular collapse or injury during the recovery period, may also be greater for an aged horse. While an otherwise vigorous and active animal may be a good candidate for the surgery, there are others who would be better served by finding them a good home where the exercise demands would not be so great.

OTHER RESPIRATORY PROBLEMS

There are other abnormalities and/or malformations of the upper respiratory tract that can cause problems for older horses. These include problems related to abnormally small or narrow nostrils and/or nasal passages, malformations of the nasal septum, and problems with the soft palate that interfere with breathing. All of the above would have been present for the life of the horse. While they themselves do not worsen just because he is older, the irritation they cause can be more significant as a predisposing factor to infections or to complications in a horse who is battling chronic lung disease. While surgical remedies are available for many of these problems, the most sane approach with an older horse usually turns out to be recognition of the problem(s) and adjustment in his exercise schedule as needed.

CANCER

Finally, increasing age always raises the question of cancer. The horse is virtually free of the cancers that originate in lung tissue that plague people. However, the lung and/or pleural lining of the chest cavity may become involved in bodywide cancers such as lymphosarcoma. This usually occurs in an animal who is obviously affected by a terminal and extensive disease process rather than as an ill-defined problem of the respiratory tract, and treatment is neither indicated nor available.

In summary, problems with the respiratory tract may be a significant consideration for the aged horse. They range from an increasing suscep-tibility to new infections to complications arising from deep-seated ab-scess formation that followed disease as a foal. Chronic problems with heaves or problems related to structural malformations can be expected to worsen and become irreversible with time. However, there are many treatment options available to relieve symptoms and eliminate or slow the progression of disease. Appropriate medical intervention when com-bined with adjustments in management and exercise requirements can result in a long, comfortable, and productive life for the horse with respi-ratory disease.

10

The Urinary Tract

*P*roblems with the urinary tract are so rare that many people own horses and work around horses their entire lives without ever seeing it. What many "old-timers" think is kidney trouble is really soreness of the back muscles related to lameness in the hock or stifle with secondary soreness along the back.

Tumors of the kidneys or bladder have been reported and, although extremely unlikely, should always be on the list of differential diagnoses when dealing with an older horse with urinary problems. Far more likely, however, is the one significant problem that horses do develop: urinary calculi ("stones").

The signs of urinary calculi are referable to the irritation caused by the stones and to blockage of the flow of urine. These include abdominal pain—often mistaken for colic from intestinal causes—blood in the urine, straining to urinate, frequent interruptions in the stream of urine, weak stream of urine, reluctance to urinate (caused by pain), and dangling of the penis in the male or winking of the vaginal lips in the female.

The urine of normal horses contains a large amount of calcium carbonate crystals. Stones will not form, however, unless there are contributing problems. These include low-grade infections, vitamin A deficiency, and possibly some dietary factors such as excess phosphorus. Of these, low-grade infection is the most common cause. Conversely, the irritation of bladder stones and the inability to empty the bladder completely usually result in infection of the bladder or upper urinary tract, which must also be treated.

The first step in therapy is to administer drugs that cause relaxation of the urethra to help the stone pass, to force fluids (unless there is complete obstruction to the flow of urine), and to administer antibiotics to treat any concurrent infection. In mares, it is sometimes possible for a veterinarian with small hands to dilate the urethra sufficiently to actually remove the stone by hand.

If the stone(s) is not passed after a few days of conservative therapy and/or if multiple large stones that cannot fit through the urethra are present in the bladder, surgery is necessary.

Geldings and stallions are more likely to have problems with urinary calculi because their urethra is longer, more tortuous, and narrower than that of a mare. Mares, on the other hand, are more likely to develop stones in the first place because foaling and breeding are associated with an increased risk of bladder infection, as are certain conformational abnormalities (see Chapter 13, "Breeding the Older Horse"). In either case, since stones may take some time to reach a size that causes the horse difficulties, age does carry an increased risk.

Equally important as being aware of possible disease of the urinary tract is recognizing that other conditions may masquerade as urinary problems. These include back soreness (as mentioned earlier), colic from intestinal causes, and tying up.

With back pain, the horse may show marked tenderness in the general area of the kidneys—along the spine in the area between the saddle and the rise of the hips. However, the more specific indicators of straining to urinate, dribbling urine, and discolored urine will be absent.

Colic of intestinal origin will also cause abdominal pain indicated by the horse's glancing at his flanks and standing rigidly. Colic can also be associated with a reluctance to urinate as this act requires generating abdominal pressure that could be painful. It is also common to see dangling of the penis in horses with colic. However, rectal examination and close physical examination will usually detect abnormalities of the intestinal tract, and the urine itself will be normal.

Finally, tying up—a condition of severe muscular spasm and muscle breakdown associated with exercise—is easily confused with urinary-tract disease. The general attitude and appearance of the horse is identical on superficial examination, and the urine may be discolored from red to brown secondary to muscle pigment. However, urinalysis can easily reveal the presence of blood versus muscle pigment and may show other abnormalities associated with urinary-tract disease, and close clinical examination will reveal if the horse has widespread muscle tenderness.

In conclusion, while urinary-tract disease does occur, it is very rare. There are other significant problems that may mimic urinary-tract conditions, all of which require veterinary attention. Never let anyone tell you the horse just has "sore kidneys" or "a cold in his kidneys," and never put off veterinary attention in favor of homemade or over-the-counter kidney remedies.

11

Arthritis

T he number-one medical problem of aged horses is arthritis. Very few indeed, if any, can reach late-middle or old age without having significant problems with arthritis at some point.

Arthritis literally means inflammation of the joint. There are many different types of arthritis, but only two of these are found in the horse— degenerative arthritis and septic arthritis. Septic arthritis is inflammation of the joint secondary to bacterial (or viral) infection, while degenerative arthritis refers to damage a joint sustains simply as a result of long-term wear and tear, or secondary to fractures or other abnormalities in the joint.

SEPTIC ARTHRITIS

Septic arthritis is certainly not a problem restricted to older horses. In fact, it is most likely to occur in very young foals who develop bodywide bacterial infections (such as strangles—*Streptococcus equi* infection). Infection may also gain access to the joint trough a wound—either an accidental injury or a surgical wound, even a needle puncture. Although the older horse is at no greater risk for septic arthritis than any other horse, it must always be remembered that septic arthritis can occur any time a joint is entered, even by a veterinarian and under as sterile conditions as possible. Joint infections are extremely difficult to treat, often requiring surgery and long-term administration of expensive antibiotics. Even when the actual infection can be cleared, there is often permanent and extensive damage to the joint. This risk must be considered when weighing the possible benefits and drawbacks of treating degenerative arthritis by intra-articular (into the joint) medications of any type.

DEGENERATIVE ARTHRITIS

Degenerative arthritis severe enough to cause clinical symptoms of lameness becomes more likely as the horse ages. In fact, it is so common that veterinary radiologists recognize a certain level of arthritic change as "normal" or "appropriate for age" when they see it in particular high-risk areas, such as the navicular bone. These aging changes occur as a direct result of wear and tear on the joint during the horse's lifetime. They will appear sooner, and be more severe, if the horse has been used hard throughout his life, particularly if his work has included work at speed and/or jumping. Other factors that contribute to the development of arthritis include imperfect conformation (even slight malalignment of the bones being significant—see Chapter 1, "Purchasing an Older Horse"), improper trimming and shoeing that also result in improper alignment of the bones of the leg, direct injury to a joint—such as a fracture—poor conditioning, and poor nutrition.

Since most horses must be athletically active to be considered worth owning, some degree of arthritis is inevitable. However, it is possible to minimize the problem by paying careful attention to the contributing factors and by exercising great care in evaluating the conformation of any aged horse being considered for purchase. The degree of any arthritic change should also be considered when deciding to purchase an animal for breeding, or to retire one to breeding, as the stress of pain can cause an overall decrease in condition that makes breeding more difficult. Mares in particular should be evaluated carefully since the added weight of pregnancy often causes severe arthritic flare-ups and there is some suspicion that the hormonal changes may also exacerbate arthritis.

PHYSIOLOGY OF ARTHRITIS

To understand the significance of arthritis changes a little better, it is important to realize that joints have a very limited ability to heal themselves. The pain of arthritis is caused either by holes (erosions) in the cartilage lining joints or by pressure and pinching from overgrowths of bone that form on the edges of an arthritic joint. These bony growths are commonly referred to as "calcium" or "spurs," and their medical term is "osteophytes."

Cartilage receives all its nutrition from the joint fluid, which is produced by tissues lining the joint. When an injury occurs, the blood supply to the tissues that produce joint fluid (the synovial membrane) increases and so does the production of fluid. However, the fluid shows abnormalities in viscosity (thickness), protein amount and type, and fluid chemistry. It also contains a large number of white blood cells. The white blood cells function to clean up the damaged area but can also create their own damaging effects. The cartilage heals very slowly, if at all, and never really recovers the same lubricating and protecting properties it had before the injury, meaning the joint will always be compromised.

Similarly, once osteophytes have formed there is really no way to eliminate them. A surgeon can file them down, but the inflammation created by the surgery itself all but guarantees that they will reform, often worse than before the procedure.

Arthritis is a significant problem because arthritic changes are irreversible and it is inevitable that athletic, active animals will eventually suffer from it.

There is some exciting research being done on the treatment of arthritis that could eventually greatly improve the quality of life for older horses. Cartilage from the sternum ("breast bone") has been surgically placed into joints with cartilage damage on an experimental basis with very promising results. These cartilage "grafts" stimulate regrowth of normal joint cartilage, which is something that has previously been considered impossible. The future may hold the closest thing yet to a "cure" for arthritis.

Any joint may become the site of arthritic change. However, the joints of the lower legs (knee and hock and below) are most likely to be affected as they must bear more weight on a small surface area and are deprived of the benefits of having large amounts of surrounding muscle to help protect them from excessive motion. The closer the joint is to the ground and the more leeway its structure has for excessive movement, the more likely arthritis will be.

NAVICULAR DISEASE

Beginning at the bottom then, the most likely area for arthritis change would be in the navicular area. As Figure 12 shows, the navicular bone is a small bone that is tucked in behind the second phalanx (part of the pastern) and the third phalanx (the coffin bone) and forms part of the joint between the two. It is held in place by a number of ligaments that form a sling. On top of the bone and ligaments is a fluid-filled bursa, and on top of this runs the deep flexor tendon. The navicular bone can be

Figure 12. Anatomy of the Foot and Pastern

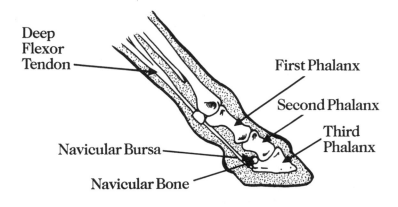

Deep Flexor Tendon

First Phalanx

Second Phalanx

Third Phalanx

Navicular Bursa

Navicular Bone

stressed from either pressure on the joint or by pressure of the deep flexor tendon on its bursa. In addition, any imbalance to the foot across the heels will pull the navicular sling out of alignment from side to side. Finally, even when the navicular is situated neatly inside a healthy, perfectly balanced foot, it is subjected to some degree of vibration and pounding (concussion) every time the foot hits the ground, and this of course is worst when the horse is moving at speed or landing after a jump.

It should be fairly obvious by now why the navicular is so commonly involved in arthritic changes and why radiologists have actually come to consider certain abnormalities of the navicular as "normal" for the age of the horse. These changes will directly reflect how hard and/or fast the horse has been worked. While some changes are always to be expected, it is possible to minimize the amount of punishment the navicular takes by always trimming the foot properly and leaving an adequate length of heel. Figure 13 shows a back view of a navicular bone that has a spur formation on one side. This change is common in horses that land unevenly and stress one side of the foot more than the other by landing only on one side.

Other changes in the navicular bone seen on X-rays include the development of large round holes in the body of the bone that correspond to blood vessels that have enlarged secondary to inflammation. This type of change is directly related to the degree of concussion on the area and

Figure 13. Navicular Disease with Spur, Bottom View

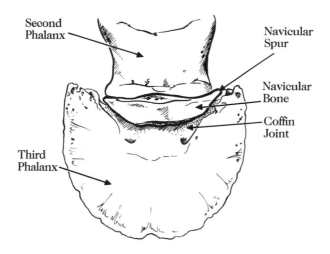

Second Phalanx

Navicular Spur

Navicular Bone

Coffin Joint

Third Phalanx

is likely to be most severe in horses who race and jump, particularly when the heels are trimmed short and the toe left long—a common practice when it is considered desirable to increase the horse's stride length. This type of trimming is damaging because it deprives the bones of the foot of the support they would normally receive from the heels by both shortening the heels and positioning them too far forward.

Finally, the total force exerted on the navicular area is related to both the speed and weight of the horse. This is why navicular disease is a problem with the front legs, which bear approximately 60 percent of the horse's weight. It also explains why navicular disease is more common and more severe in overweight horses, particularly those with very tiny feet (e.g., many show-quality Quarter Horses have been deliberately bred to have small feet and as a result suffer an inordinate amount of navicular disease).

The signs of navicular disease include a shortened, almost mincing gait in front and a tendency to put the toe down first to avoid both weight in the heels and the stretch through the deep flexor tendon that compresses the navicular against the other bones. In time, the heel area becomes very narrow as a result of the horse's desire not to use it for weight bearing. Hoof testers applied across the heels commonly elicit pain, while nerve blocks to the posterior part of the foot cause the horse to go sound. Finally, diagnosis is confirmed by X-rays, which also help to determine how severe the disease really is and if there is any sign of present or impending fracture through the navicular bone.

Treatment of Navicular Disease

Since arthritis can never be "cured," the most effective treatments are those that begin early in the course of the disease, before the irreversible changes have become too advanced. Treatment aims to eliminate pain and correct any contributing factors, thus minimizing the progression of the disease.

Humane treatment of the horse is not the only reason to aggressively pursue pain relief (although it certainly is enough reason!). Truly effective pain relief usually also involves the elimination of inflammation. Drugs such as "bute" (phenylbutazone) and any other common antiarthritis medication are both good analgesics and anti-inflammatory agents. This is important as inflammation, while important in "cleaning up" damaged areas in the joint, also creates a certain amount of damage of its own. Pain relief also leads to the resumption of a more normal gait, which helps restore health of the hoof and prevent injuries in other areas that can be caused because of the faulty gait itself.

Trimming and Shoeing

The first step in treatment must be a detailed evaluation of the horse's conformation. The worst conformation for navicular disease is that of short, upright pasterns and small feet. Such horses suffer a great deal of concussion on landing. However, long, extremely sloping pasterns can result in excessive strain on the deep flexor tendon and a foot placed too far forward, which can also strain the navicular area. Finally, observe if the horse stands with his toes straight, pointed out, or pointed in. The reason for making these observations is to determine if the horse is properly trimmed with his hoof at the proper angle to be in alignment with the other bones of his lower leg and with the foot landing squarely, not to either side.

The method of evaluating the alignment of the lower leg is described in detail in Chapter 2 (see Figure 1). Primarily, we are interested in seeing a straight line from the middle of the fetlock through the point of the toe (or wherever the horse is breaking over) and a similarly straight line from the middle of the fetlock through all the bones of the lower leg on the side view. If radiographs are available, these can be very useful in evaluating how the bones line up, particularly the side views of the foot and pastern area.

When attempting to relieve the pain of navicular disease, always start with restoring the foot to a normal alignment if the above examination shows a problem. This alone might be sufficient in early cases. If the foot is already properly balanced, the next step is to raise the angle of the foot either by leaving the heels longer at the next trimming or by placing on pads that are higher at the heels (degree pads). This relieves the pressure of the deep flexor tendon on the navicular area. It is also helpful to square off the point of the toe so that the horse can break over more easily. This decreases the amount of time that the deep flexor tendon is in full stretch, i.e., the phase when the foot is flat on the ground but the leg and body are beginning to move forward. Squaring the point of the toe on the shoes is a minimal adjustment that the blacksmith may be able to make easily just using his hammer; it will not add significantly to the cost of your shoeing. Another change in shoeing that is relatively easy and inexpensive is the addition of full pads to absorb some of the concussion.

In many cases, correction of any malalignment and one or more of the trimming and shoeing changes mentioned will be all that is necessary to relieve the pain of navicular disease and slow its progression. It is important to recognize that raising the angle, adding the weight of pads, and squaring the toe all will probably result in a shorter stride and higher action in the knees, which should not be confused with a lameness or soreness. If the above measures are not sufficient, or if the lameness reappears in time, special navicular shoes will be needed.

Navicular shoes achieve the same ends as the earlier measures discussed above, i.e., they raise the angle of the foot and provide for rapid breakover. Navicular shoes are thicker at the heels than at the toes and have a rounded surface at the toe. They are usually used with full pads, and a special soft acrylic material can be placed between the bottom of the foot and the pad to provide even more of a cushion. The main advantage of navicular shoes is that they accomplish immediately what could take weeks or longer to do with trimming alone.

Pain Medication

Proper trimming and shoeing is the cornerstone to long-term successful treatment of navicular disease. However, there will be times when it is necessary to use medication to achieve rapid relief of pain and inflammation. Phenylbutazone ("bute") is the most frequently used drug and is the standard against which all analgesic and anti-inflammatory agents should be measured. Phenylbutazone is available in intravenous and various oral preparations (pills, granules, or paste). It is very effective and lasts long enough that administration once daily is usually sufficient. The drug is well tolerated by horses, and side effects (primarily irritation of the gastrointestinal tract) are usually only a problem when the horse is on a prolonged period of treatment (weeks or months of regular use). It is also inexpensive.

Phenylbutazone is commonly used in the initial stages of the treatment of navicular disease, when attempts are being made to find the proper trimming and shoeing combinations for the horse. Once pain has been relieved, medication will only be necessary during times of flare-up, usually associated with a heavy period of work, and it is best not to rely on this or any other medication beyond a period of one week or so. Pain that persists beyond this point may indicate that a change in shoeing is needed or that the horses activity level will have to be decreased.

Neurectomy

The final treatment option for navicular disease is neurectomy or "nerving"—cutting of the nerves that supply sensation to the navicular area (and serve the skin of the back of the pastern and approximately the back half of the hoof.) The surgery itself is fairly simple and could even be

Thumbs are resting over the locations of the paired posterior digital nerves that are cut during a neurectomy ("nerving") for navicular disease pain relief.

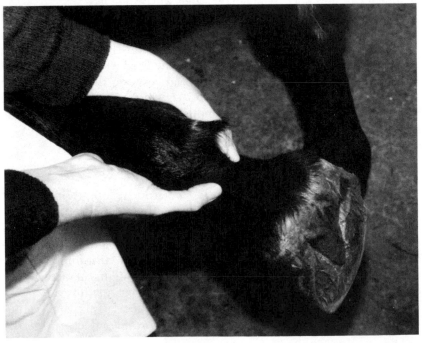

done with the horse standing, although this is not the ideal situation. A successful surgery will relieve pain permanently.

The drawbacks to neurectomy lie in aftereffects and possible complications. When deprived of sensation to half his foot, the horse may show an increased tendency to stumble, although this tends to improve in time. It is not true that horses that have had a neurectomy are dangerous to ride—in fact, a fair number of such horses even race. More serious is the possibility that the horse may develop an infection or other problem but show no signs because the normal defense warning system of pain has been eliminated. Nerved horses always should have special attention given to their feet, which should be inspected a minimum of once daily. Another possible complication is that the deep flexor tendon could rupture, causing an irreversible lameness that usually requires that the horse be euthanized. One reason the tendon can rupture is that it is often inflamed and damaged in the area of the navicular bone when navicular disease is advanced. There is also the possibility that cutting the nerve supply has an effect on normal blood flow that compromises the health of the foot.

Other complications after nerving include the possibility that the nerve supply could grow back or that painful growths called neuromas may form at the out ends of the nerves. Neuroma formation is least likely when the surgery was performed quickly and under sterile, ideal conditions (with the horse under general anesthesia in a properly equipped operating room). There is some evidence that a surgical technique of removing a piece of the nerves and then freezing the cut ends is associated with the least likelihood of neuroma formation.

Therefore, before deciding upon neurectomy, it is advisable to exhaust the other avenues of therapy. It is also necessary that a firm commitment be made to faithfully caring for the horse's feet after neurectomy. Finally, while neurectomy will most likely be reserved for the most severe cases, it should not be done if the navicular bone is fractured, or in imminent danger of fracturing, as this indicates the disease is very advanced and rupture of the flexor tendon could easily occur. These last mentioned cases should probably be euthanized.

Injection of Steroids

One final therapy for navicular disease should be mentioned. This is the injection of steroids into the area of the navicular bone in hopes of quieting the arthritis. This treatment is temporary at best and is associated with a risk of introducing deep infection into the foot. Another possible complication is weakening of the bones and joints of the area. For these reasons, it is rarely if ever indicated. One possible exception might be in a horse who has minimal or no changes in the navicular bone on X-rays but shows other clinical signs of pain in this area. Such a horse is probably in the very early stages of the disease, and the pain is primarily originating from inflammation of the navicular bursa rather than any advanced arthritis. In this case it could be beneficial to stop the inflammation as quickly as possible by using the local injection of steroids in combination with the necessary adjustments in shooing and trimming. Even then, however, there is little to be gained over giving the steroids or other anti-inflammatory drugs orally or intravenously, and the local injection will still carry a risk of infection.

FETLOCK ARTHRITIS

Another area commonly involved in arthritis is the fetlock or "ankle." The fetlock is designed to have considerable range of motion and functions as a shock absorber for the leg. The sesamoid bones are located in the back of the fetlock joint and are suspended in a slinglike arrangement of ligaments, much the same as the navicular bone. Arthritis starts when the fetlock is repeatedly overstressed, as in work at speed or when landing over a jump. This causes overstretching of the supporting ligaments and joint capsule, which inflames the bone. The bones are also forced up tightly against each other and may even travel beyond the normal limits of the joint surface. Repeated compressions of the joint will

**Figure 14. Anterior View of the Fetlock Showing
Degenerative Joint Disease**

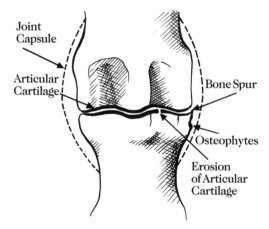

eventually cause the cartilage to wear thin and can lead to erosions in its surface, while bones that travel beyond the normal cartilage-lined joint surfaces are then rubbing bone against bone, leading to the formation of osteophytes or small fractures (see Figure 14).

There are no specific shoeing techniques that are "corrective" for arthritis above the foot, but there are some factors that contribute to stress in this area. Horses who have very long and sloping pasterns tend to have a great deal of motion in the area of the fetlock. This is what gives them such a pleasant, smooth ride, but it also places a great strain on the joint. Work at speed or over jumps and excessive weight compound the stress. Horses who toe out or toe in will have an additional stress on one side of the fetlock (see discussion in Chapter 1, "Purchasing an Older Horse"). Shoeing that places the heels too far forward, results in very short heels, or attempts to bring the foot back under the body when the horse's normal conformation would be to toe in or out, worsen these stresses (see Chapter 2, "Routine Health Care"—Trimming and Shoeing). Also, devices such as grabs, caulks, or borium applied to the shoes cause them to grab more firmly. This can result in the fetlock twisting and jerking over what is basically a fixed foot during part of the stride. Therefore, the horse with arthritic changes in his fetlocks should be shod with a flat shoe whenever possible and trimmed to have a normal angle and heel length.

ARTHRITIS OF KNEES AND HOCKS

Two other common areas for arthritic change are the knees and hocks. Arthritis of the knees is most common in horses who have raced, although poor conformation can lead to this problem in any horse. Arthritis of the hocks may develop secondary to poor conformation (particularly legs that are overly straight, jumping, quick starts and stops, pulling, collected work, or work over hilly ground.

As with the fetlock, there are no specific shoeing techniques with arthritis of the knees or hocks. It is important though to make certain the foot is trimmed properly to avoid uneven stress on the legs and to avoid grabs, caulks, or borium studs as much as possible to decrease the likelihood of wrenching the joints.

BACK PROBLEMS

Swayback

The caricature of older horses as sway-backed has a basis in truth. With age comes a weakening of the back, which could exacerbate existing back problems or cause new ones.

The back weakening is caused by a combination of factors. The sum effect of the pull of gravity over many years causes the back to sag downward. This effect is enhanced as the various ligaments holding the spine in proper alignment weaken as a result of aging. Similarly, the supporting muscles that run parallel to the spine lose mass as the animal ages. There is very little you can do about the natural effects of aging and gravity. However, the onset and severity of back weakening is perhaps more powerfully influenced by external factors that you definitely can do something about.

Excessive body weight and loss of conditioning will accelerate the onset of back weakness. It becomes increasingly difficult to avoid an older horse becoming overweight if his general health and dental care are good, but careful attention to the horse's weight will protect the integrity of his topline far longer. If you intend the older horse to be used to any degree, it is also important to maintain a regular, year round exercise program. This is because muscle strength lost in the later years will most likely never be regained, even on proper conditioning programs. Remember that the older horse does not move around and play as much as a younger animal and turn out alone will not maintain his condition.

Back Pain

If the horse has a history of back problems, it is particularly important to maintain a regular exercise program as failure to do so may result in the onset of severe back pain. We have very little information regarding the prevalence of spinal problems such as degenerative arthritis, disc disease, or spinal stenosis in horses. This is more the result of the strength of X-ray equipment and the horse's size limiting the ability to study the spine of the horse than to any real certainty that these conditions do not exist. In fact, it would be foolish to assume that horses do not have spinal problems that humans and other species can be troubled by.

It is always best to assume the horse with back pain has a genuine back problem, not a "secondary" problem caused by another lameness (which is a diagnosis all too often made). The key to long term management of such horses is weight control and maintenance of proper conditioning, including generous amounts of lateral work and bending. Particularly disastrous are sudden weight gains or periods of inactivity that strain the back and weaken the muscles and ligaments supporting the spine. If there is a skeletal problem at the root of the problem (e.g., spinal stenosis, a narrowing), or a disc problem, the loss of support will only make the problem worse.

When pain flares, treatment with massage and heat is very helpful.

DMSO-dimethylsulfoxide, liniments, and "rubs" are also very useful but care must be taken to avoid skin irritation in the saddle area. The back musculature can also be injected with corticosteroids or counterirritant drugs (iodine based) for good relief of pain. I personally use a technique that combines injection of acupuncture points and all areas of pain with serrapin, which is an extract of the pitcher plant.

ANTIARTHRITIS DRUGS

Medical treatment of arthritis in the fetlock and other joints is basically of two types—drugs that nonspecifically relieve pain and inflammation and drugs that are designed to work within the joint fluid itself. Again, phenylbutazone is the primary analgesic and anti-inflammatory drug. Other such drugs include the steroids and the nonsteroidal anti-inflammatory drugs such as Banamine, Arquel, or Equiproxen. There are advantages and disadvantages to each of these drugs, and your veterinarian, who is most familiar with the horse, is the best person to advise which to use and when. It is important to remember that these drugs do not cure arthritis and none should be used continuously for long periods of time. Their proper use is in controlling pain and inflammation during a flare-up of the disease.

The other category of drugs is designed for injection directly into the joint. The drug that has been used the longest is hyaluronic acid. This is a complex protein that is normally found in joint fluid and plays a large part in keeping the joint well-lubricated. This in turn reduces friction and inflammation, minimizing wear on the cartilage and pain from any lesions already present. Most recently, compounds have been introduced that actually attach to the site of erosions in the cartilage, protect them, and seem to speed healing.

Although more work needs to be done on the long-term effectiveness of these antiarthritic injections, they truly do seem to be wonder drugs. Improvement is seen in very close to 100 percent of horses treated, with a sizeable percentage being completely sound after therapy. Since infection is always a risk when a joint is entered, strictly sterile technique is necessary when doing the injection. Another drawback is cost, which will usually run several hundred dollars. Nevertheless, results are remarkable and response usually lasts several months. These treatments can restore an active, even competitive, lifestyle to many horses who would otherwise have been retired or put down.

Steroids have also been used intra-articularly to treat arthritis. Unfortunately, the risk of infection is very high with these compounds and repeated injections can cause the bone to weaken. This treatment is

Two common sites of localized muscle tenderness in horses with arthritis in the lower joints of the hind leg.

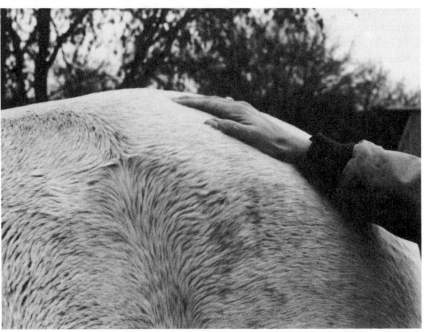

also relatively short-lived in effectiveness when compared to the newer drugs and should probably be avoided except in very special circumstances.

REST AND PHYSICAL THERAPY

Finally, a large part of successful therapy in arthritis cases is the use of rest or controlled exercise and physical therapy. Regardless of the drug therapy and trimming and/or shoeing techniques chosen, it is often imperative that the stress to the joint be stopped in the early phases of treatment. Stall rest or turnout may be advised for periods anywhere from several days to several weeks, depending upon the therapy. The shortest rest periods are associated with the new intra-articular therapies. Rest is critical to getting the inflammation under control, as any drug may fail if it must try to work in the face of continued heavy exercise.

While rest is important to quieting down an inflamed arthritic joint, excessive periods of inactivity can cause loss of physical condition or the development of stiffness in the joint. For this reason, it may be recommended that you give the horse a short period of complete rest and then begin with a controlled exercise program that will be tailor-made to the condition. For example, a horse with arthritic hocks cannot stand a lot of jumping, sharp turns, hill work, or collected work when he is suffering a flare-up of his disease. While walking and cantering will benefit his overall condition, he may still develop a stiffness as it is very easy to minimize flexion of the hock at these gaits. The best program for him would be one that incorporates a fair amount (several miles) of trotting on the flat as soon as he is comfortable on the leg.

Physical therapy may seem like an odd term to apply to the horse, but there are many time-honored treatments for arthritis that fall into this category. The simplest and most beneficial is massage—what the grooms call "rubbing the horse." A brisk, ten-minute massage is extremely helpful in improving blood flow, reducing swelling and pain, and eliminating stiffness. When done with a liniment or other agent, the effects can be even better.

Liniments and Braces

The lore surrounding leg braces, paints, and blisters is extensive, and horsemen have their own favorite recipes and prescriptions. The basic categories are the liniments and braces, which cool or warm the leg; poultices (clay packs), which decrease swelling; paints, which are irritating to the skin and cause a local increase in blood flow; and blisters, which work on the same principle as the paints but are more severe.

Considerable debate surrounds the use of these preparations. There are those who hold that they are totally useless except for the fact that they force the caretaker to massage the leg or, in the case of blisters, guarantee that the horse will get a much-needed rest. On the other hand are those who strongly feel these agents are indispensable in maintaining a horse's soundness. The truth is somewhere between these two extremes.

When speaking of older horses, we are primarily dealing with a group of animals who have chronic, low-grade problems that wax and wane in severity. The goal of physical therapy must be to keep the horse comfortable enough to perform his daily activities and to avoid at all costs any prolonged period of lay-up. For this reason, the medications that are of most interest are the liniments and braces.

Liniments and braces work for horses on the same principle as Ben-Gay does for human beings. The combination of massage and the chemicals in the compounds causes a local reaction of heat and increased blood flow that eases pain and stiffness. The more vigorous the massage, the more marked the effect. There are too many preparations available to go into each in detail. Your veterinarian can recommend a good commercially available compound or may prefer to mix one for you.

One component that merits special mention is DMSO—dimethylsulfoxide. This drug is a by-product of petroleum manufacturing and has unique properties. Alone, it penetrates the skin and causes considerable warmth, partially by breaking up water bonds. This in turn greatly helps to reduce swelling. DMSO can also carry certain drugs through the skin and is commonly mixed with steroids such as prednisone to achieve low levels of the steroid in tissues. DMSO is usually very effective in relieving pain and swelling but must be used more carefully than most other liniments, braces, or sweats. It can cause hair loss and blistering of the skin in sensitive horses if applied over a particularly inflamed area and/or under a bandage. This is primarily a problem with chestnuts, but it can occur in any horse. It is also recommended that you wear gloves when applying DMSO to avoid getting repeated doses yourself. DMSO comes in liquid or gel form.

Massage and Bandaging

Every owner of an arthritic older horse should learn the proper technique for massaging a leg and applying a bandage. Successful massage consists of five to ten minutes of brisk rhythmical rubbing. Massage of the tendons and any affected joints should be done both before and after work for best results. You may also wish to wrap the leg after the final massage to achieve maximum comfort and benefit from the liniment.

"Yankee Clipper," a 20-year-old owned by Caroline Berry, of Zebulon, North Carolina, is receiving that little extra TLC of wrapping his legs.

These techniques, when regularly employed, will provide the horse with significant relief from pain and go a long way to preventing stiffness.

Hydrotherapy

Other therapeutic modalities that fall under the heading of physical therapy include hosing, whirlpools, and various new techniques such as electrical stimulation, ultrasound, and laser therapy. These latter treatments are very new and unfortunately not well-documented as to their effectiveness or how best to use them. However, they may be worth trying if your veterinarian is very familiar with their use and has had some success. Hydrotherapy is a time-honored approach to alleviating leg pain that is very effective. The basics are simple, with cold water being used for hot, inflamed joints and warm water for chronic stiffness and pain. The relief is the same you would experience from an ice pack on a sprained ankle or a good soak in the tub for a sore back. A minimum of ten minutes is required for good results. The horse may be soaked in a special boot or tub, hosed, or stood in a whirlpool specially designed to treat horses. Maximum benefit is achieved with two to three treatments per day followed by massage and bandaging (if necessary).

Arthritis is a fact of life for most older horses. Many of the changes of arthritis are irreversible, but a good treatment program can go a long way toward alleviating pain and slowing the progression of the disease. Every horse should be carefully evaluated to guarantee that the trimming and shoeing techniques used on him are appropriate and providing the maximum benefit. Physical therapy techniques of massage and hydrotherapy are also appropriate for any arthritic horse and provide significant pain relief while helping to prevent stiffness. Finally, drug therapy with anti-inflammatory and analgesic agents can provide relief during flare-ups, and the new antiarthritis drugs designed for injection directly into the joint show great promise in restoring usefulness to horses who previously would have been retired or euthanized.

ADVANCES IN JOINT SURGERY
AND DIAGNOSIS OF ARTHRITIS

One of the problems in obtaining a satisfactory treatment in arthritis cases is the difficulty in deciding upon what treatment options are the best. To do this, the veterinarian needs detailed information about the condition of the joint, much more information than is available on X-rays.

Today, using the arthroscope (similar to the endoscope used to check the throat and upper respiratory system of the horse), it is possible to get a direct look at the interior of a horse's joint by making only very small incisions (called stab incisions) that allow the introduction of the arthroscope and any needed instruments. The veterinarian will then know exactly how much, if any, joint cartilage is involved and can check all the internal structures for injury or inflammation. Risks of arthroscopic surgery/examination are very low compared to those for actually opening a joint through a "classical" surgical approach.

It is also possible to perform the vast majority of needed surgical procedures using the laparoscope and laparoscopic instruments. Repair or removal of fractures and a wide variety of other procedures can all be done in this manner. Procedures that veterinarians were not likely to do in the past, including removing inflamed or diseased synovial linings in a joint, can now be done with more confidence that the benefit is likely to outweigh the chance of complications of surgery.

All complications and side effects are reduced by this approach. Risk of infection and hemorrhage is lower, total operative time is decreased, and postoperative pain is reduced. Recovery times and hospital stay are decreased. The bottom line for the owner is that the risk and cost of joint surgery are lower and the chance of a favorable outcome is greatly increased with arthroscopic surgery.

12

Tumors

T he risk of benign and cancerous tumors, and of having significant problems related to these tumors, increases with age. There
are multiple reasons for this phenomenon. One is that the growth
of tumors is controlled by a very complicated series of checks and bal-
ances in the immune system. Age carries with it, as mentioned elsewhere, a general decline in the immune system and therefore an increased
likelihood of some tumors. Also, it is believed that many tumors either
are caused by repeated exposures to agents in the environment termed
carcinogens or result many years following an infection with a tumor
virus. Finally, tumors may start growing in the younger adult years but
do not reach sufficient size or spread to cause a problem until much later.

BENIGN TUMORS

Benign tumors are characterized by slow growth and failure to spread
to other areas. Benign tumors are also sometimes called polyps or simply "growths." The most common benign tumors of horses are lipomas,
sarcoids, and nasal polyps.

Lipomas

Lipomas, as you might have guessed, are composed of fat cells. The
cause is unknown. Lipomas are usually found in the abdomen but may

occasionally form under the skin. Cutaneous (skin) lipomas are totally harmless of themselves but are unsightly and may cause a problem if located under an area of tack. Lipomas can be removed easily by surgery and, depending on the size, this can often be done under local anesthesia with the horse simply sedated. Recurrence is unlikely. Lipomas in the abdomen become problematic usually in older horses. They generally hang by a long stalk and can become wrapped around a piece of intestine and cause colic (see Chapter 7, "The Gastrointestinal Tract"). If this occurs, the only treatment is surgery. Abdominal lipomas are otherwise harmless, with very large tumors found sometimes at autopsy in a horse who never had any trouble referable to the mass.

Sarcoids

Sarcoids are irregular, bumpy skin growths caused by a virus. They are most common on the face, head, and chest but can occur anywhere. Sarcoids grow slowly unless they are located in an area where they are continually irritated (e.g., by a halter), and the tumor itself does not spread. However, since they are caused by a virus that can travel widely in the body, it is not unusual to see multiple sarcoids on a horse. Sarcoids have no harmful effects on the horses general health. However, they are unsightly, bleed easily when traumatized, and can be a problem if located under tack.

Treatment of sarcoids may be surgical or nonsurgical. The most effective surgical approach involves removing the tumor and then freezing its base to kill any remaining tumor cells. This technique has a variable success rate, depending upon the size of the tumor and its depth, but generally is successful. Difficulties can arise when tumors are located on the ears, as freezing here may damage the cartilage, or on the face, where scars are undesirable.

The nonsurgical mode of therapy may replace the older surgical procedures. A new drug has been introduced Regressin-V (Vetrepharm) that can be injected into and around the base of the tumor and causes the body to destroy it by stimulating local immunity.

The drug is a suspension made of the cell walls of the organisms the mycobacteriacae. These organisms have antitumor activity. The agent is injected at weekly intervals until full regression occurs. Most sarcoids are very sensitive to the treatment and 92 percent of horses remain tumor free after two years.

Nasal Polyps

Nasal polyps are not a specific problem of aged horses and are usually detected earlier in life as they can cause a horse to breathe noisily long before they reach the size that they seriously interfere with air flow. If not treated at this point, or if undetected early because of their location, polyps may reach a size later in life that does affect breathing and necessitate removal. Polyps must be removed surgically, and the major risk is hemorrhage during the operation, as well as the nonspecific risk factors of anesthetic reaction or injury during the recovery period. Osteoporosis, chronic lameness, chronic lung disease, and decreased cardiovascular efficiency are among the factors that add to the general risks of any surgery. Therefore, since the polyp itself will not cause the horse any general harm, it is best to leave it alone in an aged horse until and unless he is not able to breathe comfortably—regardless of how noisy his breathing might be.

Goiter

From middle age onward, horses also have an increased prevalence of tumors involving the thyroid gland. These can be easily felt, and usually readily seen, along the course of the upper third of the trachea (windpipe). There will be a firm, usually smooth and well-rounded mass just underneath the skin, obviously attached to the deeper tissues with the skin moving freely over the top of it. The vast majority of these growths are benign and cause the horse no obvious problems either clinically or detectable by studies of thyroid hormone levels. Occasionally, the enlargement may be due to goiter (which literally means enlargement of the thyroid gland) secondary to inflammation or imbalance in dietary iodine. This is most commonly seen in horses that are fed kelp or other seaweed as a supplement and was actually quite common a number of years ago when supplementation of mares with iodine was in vogue. Goiter may also be caused by a natural deficiency of iodine in the diet, as is seen in many mountainous and inland areas, including the Great Lakes Basin, the Northern Great Plains states, the upper Mississippi Valley, the Rocky Mountain states, and the Pacific Coast states of the United States.

Goiter is associated with depression of thyroid activity, which may show up as weight loss or gain (depending upon appetite), decreased reproductive efficiency, lethargy, poor hair coat, muscle weakness or tying up with exercise, anemia that fails to respond to dietary supplements, and intolerance to cold. It is treated by addition or elimination of iodine supplements, as appropriate.

CANCEROUS TUMORS

The horse is also subject to a variety of cancerous tumors, i.e., tumors that grow more rapidly than benign tumors and can invade other body sites and cause death.

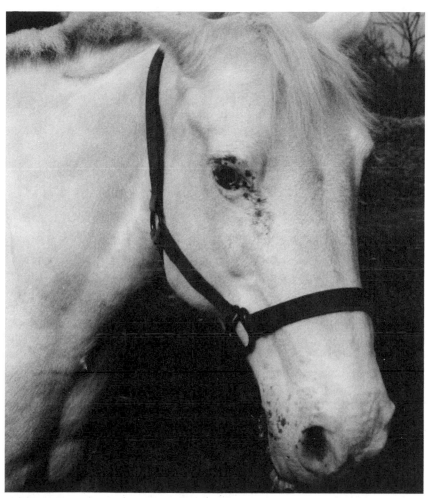

Older grey horses are at high risk for the development of malignant melanoma. Happily, our model ("Angel," a 20-year-old mare from Thorncroft Equestrian Center) is free of disease but must be watched closely for this problem.

Malignant Melanoma

The skin is the common location for two types of cancers (malignancies): malignant melanoma and squamous cell carcinoma. The malignant melanoma is limited almost exclusively to gray horses and will affect a very large percentage as they age. Melanomas usually begin on the skin in the anal and tail area. They are hard, rounded bumps that gradually increase in size. The tumor is not very invasive but can slowly spread to involve the deeper tissues of the pelvis, abdomen, and abdominal lymph nodes. There are usually no particular problems associated with melanoma unless the growths become very large and interfere with intestinal function, the spine, or with movement of the legs. In rare cases they may spread to the lungs or other sites.

Surgical removal may be attempted in very early cases, but this would be for purely cosmetic reasons and is generally not done. There is also a possibility that surgery may release tumor cells into the blood stream and cause more rapid spread. While still experimental, recent research has shown that the drug cimetidine can cause long term regression of troublesome melanomas.

Squamous Cell Carcinoma

Squamous cell carcinoma is a fairly common cancer in horses. It is most commonly located at the junction of the skin and a mucus membrane, that is, around the mouth or nose, and is also frequently found on the head of the penis and around the eye. Squamous cell carcinoma spreads to distant sites very slowly but causes a great deal of local damage. The treatment is surgical removal of the tumor, with or without radiation treatment afterward. Radiation is usually administered by implanting small radioactive "seeds" into the tumor bed and requires hospitalization with special isolation precautions. Success rates are highest when the tumor is detected early. Any unusual growth, ulcerated area, or unusual bleeding should be investigated promptly.

Fortunately, squamous cell carcinoma is very slow to spread beyond the site of its initial appearance. Since it usually occurs at a highly visible location, success rates with therapy are very high, best results being obtained with surgical removal followed by radiation therapy. Any recurrence of disease can be treated in the same manner with no decrease in the probability of success (i.e., probably no increased likelihood that the tumor has spread elsewhere even if you are dealing with a recurrence of disease). The decision of whether or not to treat is usually based more on considerations of cost and/or disfigurement after therapy than on whether or not the disease has progressed to an inevitably fatal phase.

Squamous cell carcinoma may also involve the deeper tissues of the mouth and has been found in the stomach. Because of delays in detection, success rates are far lower and surgery is usually not recommended.

Fibrosarcoma

There are a variety of other tumors of the mouth, throat, nasal cavity, and sinuses. These include fibrosarcomas and other types of carcinoma.

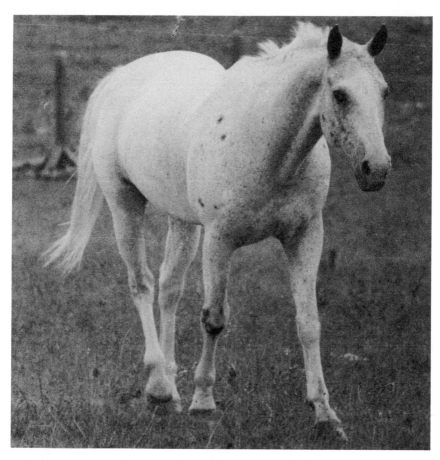

Lgihtly pigmented horses, like this 16-year-old Appaloosa gelding, "Lightning Deck," owned by Debbie Grice, of Clarksville, Tennessee, is at higher risk for developing squamous cell carcinoma around the eyes and face.

They are quite invasive locally and usually have caused considerable damage before they are detected. Swallowing difficulties may be the first obvious sign, although careful palpation at that time usually reveals an obvious mass(es). No treatment is recommended in most cases.

Ovarian Tumors

With the exception of the squamous cell carcinomas in the stomach mentioned above, tumors of the intestinal tract are virtually nonexistent. The horse is very different from man in this respect. The abdomen may harbor lipomas as described earlier. Other abdominal tumors include ovarian tumors and the very rare case of tumor in the kidneys, spleen, or liver. Although these tumors are definitely malignant, they tend to be very slow-growing and may never be detected unless they erode through a major blood vessel and cause hemorrhage or become so large that movement causes discomfort. Ovarian tumors have been reported that are basketball size or even larger.

The only abdominal tumor (with the exception of lipomas) that is readily removed surgically is the ovarian tumor. This can even be done with the mare standing and is usually attempted if she is having trouble with abdominal pain or if the tumor is impinging on the urinary tract or bowel. Success rates are very high.

Brain Tumors

Older horses are particularly susceptible to tumors of the brain. These are usually located in the area of the pituitary gland and cause a dramatic clinical picture. The pituitary gland is the "control gland" for the body. The function of all the other glands—thyroid, adrenal glands, reproductive glands, parathyroid gland—are controlled by hormones secreted by the pituitary. The most common sign of pituitary tumor is a very long hair coat that the horse never sheds. Other signs depend upon which areas of the pituitary are affected and may include blood-sugar abnormalities (diabetes millitus), electrolyte and fluid disturbances (diabetes insipidus), calcium and phosphorus imbalances (parathyroid gland), and excessive weight gain with fatigue and muscle weakness (thyroid). The only surgical approach to the pituitary gland is through the roof of the mouth. The anatomy of the horses head makes this very delicate surgery difficult to impossible in the horse. Even if it were possible, the horse's advanced age and the advanced stage of disease by the time the problem is brought to the attention of a veterinarian dictate that no treatment be attempted. Horses with pituitary tumors will show a slow but steady downhill course with muscle wasting, weight loss, weakness, insatiable thirst, and abnormalities of the blood chemistry with an eventual natural death related to failure of multiple organ systems. Euthanasia is always indicated once this diagnosis is made.

Cancer of the Reticuloendothelial System

The final malignancy of horses to be considered is cancer of the reticuloendothelial system. The reticuloendothelial system is a bodywide network of special tissues responsible in large part for the functioning of the immune system. It includes the lymph nodes, the spleen, the lymphatic vessels (a network similar to the veins that connects the various lymph nodes in the body), and reticuloendothelial tissue present diffusely in all body tissues. Several different types of malignancies can start in this system. These include the leukemias, which are characterized by abnormally high numbers of certain white bloods cells; lymphomas—localized large lymphoid tumors; and lymphosarcoma—a more widely spread lymphoid tissue tumor.

The most common, and invariably fatal, form in horses is lymphosarcoma. This malignancy spreads rapidly to involve many organ systems and the tissues lining the chest and abdominal cavities. Enlarged lymph nodes and/or tumors on the skin may be the first presentation, and there may be associated large tumors in the chest or abdomen. More commonly, however, the horse shows a rapid weight loss and fatigue with accumulation of large amounts of fluid in the abdomen and/or chest. Chemotherapy is the treatment of choice in other species, but there is no recommended therapy for horses as yet. Diagnosis is based on the microscopic appearance of biopsies taken from a tumor or of fluid removed from the chest or abdomen. Euthanasia is always indicated.

Advancing age and tumors go hand in hand. Fortunately, the overall incidence of tumors is low in horses and the most common types tend to be benign, located on the surface of the body and/or not overly invasive. Owners of older horses should always be alert to warning signs of cancer including unusual growths or swellings, ulcerated areas, slow healing, or unusual bleeding. The head is a common site for tumors, and the usual first sign here is difficulty swallowing. Tumors of the stomach may present first as an unexplained anemia secondary to slow bleeding into the digestive tract. Finally, vague difficulties in breathing or chronic, low-level abdominal pain may be due to cancer in the chest or abdomen. Veterinary consultation is indicated at the first appearance of any of these signs.

13

Breeding
the Older Horse

THE AGED BROODMARE

*I*t is not at all unusual for horses to be reproductively active well into their teens. Mares are certainly capable of producing perfectly normal foals at this age. Reproductively sound aged broodmares often have very reasonable price tags in recognition of the limited reproductive span they have remaining. These mares are experienced in raising foals, and you have the distinct advantage of being able to see firsthand the type of foals they produce. These facts often make an aged broodmare the perfect choice for someone who wishes to get started in breeding with a good mare but has limited funds. Such mares are also a good purchase for the semiserious breeder who would have continued use for the animal as a family horse even after she stopped producing foals.

There are a number of fertility problems in mares that increase in likelihood with age and the number of foals she has produced. Overall, a mare age thirteen to fifteen or older will have about a 30 percent conception rate versus 50 to 60 percent for a younger mare. Anyone purchasing an aged broodmare (or who already has a mare that develops problems) should thoroughly understand the nature of these problems and their consequences.

Daughter of "Sugar Sabre," Supreme Champion, this 20-year-old American Quarter Horse has had four foals, the most recent in spring 1992. Here, "Sandy Sugar" is having a quiet moment away from her rambunctious son, "Pete." Owned by Richard Sears, Sheds, New York. Photograph by Judy Sears.

Uterine Infections

Uterine infections are a common problem in all farm animals. As a mare ages, the ligaments supporting the external genitalia weaken. The vaginal area then begins to tilt inward (versus the normal vertical position), making air sucking and fecal contamination more likely (see page 151). Infections may be severe, with an obviously abnormal discharge and fever, or relatively mild, with the mare showing no obvious clinical signs except for some difficulty in getting back in foal or in staying in foal. Uterine infections always result in some degree of scarring of the wall of the uterus. Even the effects of mild infections will add up over time, and the end result may be a uterus that does not have sufficient normal area to support the placenta. Such problems are particularly likely in the horse as the placenta normally attaches over a larger percentage of the surface area of the uterus and there is very little uterine lining not involved in the support of a pregnancy.

The usual problem seen with uterine scarring is early abortion. The mare may seem to have conceived (e.g., failed to come back into heat and had rectal examinations compatible with pregnancy) but is found to be open (not pregnant) on the routine forty-five-day examination. Most of these mares do get pregnant, but the abnormalities in the uterus prevent the placenta from developing normally and the pregnancy is lost.

Diagnosis of uterine scarring is made by removing a small piece of the uterus with a special biopsy instrument and submitting it for microscopic examination. This is a relatively simple procedure and can be performed on most mares without any need for sedatives or anesthesia. The procedure has been around for quite some time and experienced pathologists can very accurately predict the general condition of the whole uterus from just this tiny sample. The chances of keeping a mare with uterine scarring in foal are directly related to how severe the changes are and also to the presence or absence of any other problems. While it is true that even mares who would be considered hopelessly sterile based on their biopsy results have managed to carry a foal, the chances of this happening are extremely slim. The accuracy of reproductive predictions based on uterine biopsies is generally so high that this is probably the single most informative and important test to be done with aged mares experiencing breeding problems.

Mares should also be tested for active uterine infections by culturing a sample of the fluid in the uterus. Even before the scarring develops, active infections may prevent conception by causing swelling of the tissues and changes in the fluids of the reproductive tract that interfere with the sperm and egg. Even if fertilization of the egg does occur, the egg may be unable to attach to the inflamed uterine wall and will die within a matter of days.

Culture of the uterus is a very simple procedure. A long, sterile culture tube is carefully passed through the cervix and into the uterus. Once the tube is situated, a sterile cotton swab is pushed through it and allowed to absorb the materials to be cultured. This is then withdrawn safely inside the tube and removed. Again, sedation and/or anesthesia are usually not required.

When infection is found, the organism should always be tested to see which antibiotics would be most effective. This is done by growing the organism on a culture plate together with several small paper discs that are impregnated with various antibiotics. If the organism is sensitive to one or more of the drugs, it will fail to grow in the area surrounding that particular disc. This is called sensitivity testing.

Once the appropriate drug is located, the mare is treated by instillation of a solution containing that antibiotic directly into the uterus. This is done daily for approximately four to ten days, depending on the severity of infection. It is sometimes possible to place a piece of tubing inside the uterus that can then be sutured to the skin of the vulva so that owners may do the daily infusions themselves, thus cutting some costs. However, this technique is not suitable for all mares as the tubes can become easily dislodged if the mare rubs the area or if she pulls away during the infusion.

If a severe infection is present, it may also be necessary to stimulate the uterus to contract in hopes of causing it to force out some of the infected materials. In these cases, the veterinarian will administer the drug Pitocin and possibly estrogens.

When treating uterine infections, it must always be remembered that clearing the infection is only part of the battle. The final result will also depend on how extensive the scarring changes are. Since time is of the essence when treating an aged mare, it may be advisable to have a uterine biopsy performed before even deciding to treat an infection as there may already be a significant amount of uterine scarring present.

Uterine infections result from a number of contributing factors. Many infections are acquired at foaling when the conditions within the uterus are very favorable for bacterial growth. There is certainly no way to render the foaling conditions sterile within a barn, but it is important to minimize gross contamination of the mare during this time. This is the reason behind wrapping the tail and keeping the vaginal area free of caked dirt or secretions before foaling, picking out the foaling stall regularly, using disinfectants on foaling stall walls and floors, and cleaning up the mare as soon as possible after foaling. Such measures are far from 100 percent effective, but they may help keep contamination to a level the mare can handle without becoming infected.

Mares may also develop reproductive-tract infections at other times as a result of poor conformation. In a normal mare, the vaginal lips run roughly perpendicular to the ground. However, as a result of hereditary poor conformation or aging, many mares show a tipping of the vagina that gives them an inward slant or caved-in appearance at the vagina. The seal of the vaginal lips is not very effective in such mares, with the result that air and fecal material may enter the vagina. In addition, the opening of the urinary tract—the urethra—is located inside the vagina, and mares with the abnormal conformation just described often have a problem with some urine running back toward the uterus instead of to the outside. Termed urine pooling, this also increases the likelihood of infection and/or inflammation.

There are surgical procedures to correct these problems. The simplest is a "Caslick's" operation. This involves suturing shut the top portion of the vagina and leaving just enough of an opening to allow urination (see Figure 15). It is very effective in preventing air and other materials from entering the vagina. A Caslick's, however, will not correct urine pooling, and a more complicated plastic surgery to reposition the urethra is needed in such mares.

Figure 15. Caslick's Operation with Sutures in Place

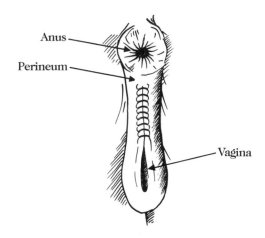

Anus

Perineum

Vagina

These surgeries are performed with the mare standing and with the use of only a local or spinal anesthetic. As mentioned, they are usually quite effective. However, before performing surgery on an aged mare it is always advisable to perform a uterine biopsy to determine the extent of any permanent damage and to culture the mare and clear any infections before proceeding with the surgical treatment.

Ovarian Activity

With older broodmares (late teens and twenties), erratic estrus cycles or complete cessation of cycling can be seen. This is the equine equivalent of menopause. Ovaries become shrunken and inactive. The only reason we do not see this with all mares is that they often die or are euthanized for unrelated reasons before it can occur. Obviously, this marks the end of the mare's reproductive life.

Pregnancy Loss

Aged mares have an overall 25 to 30 percent chance of early loss of the pregnancy, compared to about 10 percent for younger mares. Uterine scarring (see section on infections) that decreases the area available for the placenta to implant is one cause. Another factor may be death of the fetus due to chromosomal defects, which are more common as the eggs age. (All eggs are present from the time of the mare's birth.)

Another problem that can cause early death of the fetus is insufficient production of the hormone progesterone. Progesterone is essential to the maintenance of a normal pregnancy. The causes for a low level in mares is not well understood; it may occur even in mares that appear perfectly normal. Once the problem is diagnosed (through testing for hormone levels in the blood), it is possible in some cases to supplement the progesterone by intramuscular injections and save the pregnancy.

Hemorrhage of the Uterine Artery

In addition to the increased problems with getting and keeping an aged mare in foal, the higher risks of pregnancy itself must be considered.

Aged mares are more prone to suffering hemorrhage of the uterine artery during foaling. The uterine arteries are large vessels that provide the majority of the blood supply for the uterus. There are two, the left and right uterine arteries, and they travel from the aorta to the uterus through a sheet of tissue that also serves to support the uterus. These arteries grow tremendously during pregnancy to meet the demands of the placenta. With time, the walls may become weakened and the artery may rupture during foaling.

Many mares survive their first episode of uterine artery rupture because the tissues around the vessel contain the bleeding until the local pressure becomes great enough to stop it. However, mares may die the first time this happens, and the risks of losing the mare rise sharply if she becomes pregnant and experiences a rupture again.

Clinical signs of uterine-artery rupture are those of shock. The mare becomes weak, trembles, and breaks out into a sweat. If the blood loss is large, she may go down and show a weak pulse, and if hemorrhage is not controlled by pressure from the surrounding tissues she can die.

There is nothing that can be done to prevent or stop uterine-artery rupture. Treatment during an acute episode includes the administration of fluids intravenously and sometimes drugs to help support the blood pressure until the hemorrhage stops and the mare stabilizes.

The area of hemorrhage can be felt on rectal examination, and any mare known by such examination to have had a previous uterine-artery rupture should not be bred.

Pregnancy and Lameness

Pregnancy also carries other risks that, though not fatal, can seriously affect a mares health. Of primary consideration is the effect of pregnancy on chronic lamenesses.

Many mares are first retired to breeding when they develop a lameness problem. While it is true that speed work and jumping create the greatest problems for most lamenesses, the increased weight of pregnancy can also place considerable stress on chronic lamenesses. This is most likely to be a problem with foot troubles or tendon and/or ligament injuries, although other joints may be affected as well. If the pregnancy causes increased pain from such problems, the mare will move around less and is likely not to eat or drink enough. This has an adverse effect on fetus and mother alike. Some veterinarians also believe that the large shifts in hormones associated with pregnancy can worsen some types of arthritis.

To minimize or eliminate lameness complications in the broodmare, the first step must be to establish that she has minimal or no pain or problems ambulating before she is even bred. Not enough is known about the possible effects of common analgesic drugs on the fetus, while other agents (the steroid family) could make the mare more likely to abort. Therefore, the lameness should be stable and trimming and/or shoeing procedures well established prior to breeding the mare.

During pregnancy, the caretaker and/or farm manager should be well aware of any previous lameness problems a mare has had so that she can be watched closely for any signs of trouble. If she does begin to show lameness she should be removed from any large groups and maintained where she will not have to compete for food and water or deal with aggressive pasturemates. Every effort should be made to relieve the pain by adjustments in trimming and shoeing together with massage, supportive leg wraps, hydrotherapy, poultices, and liniments rather than resorting immediately to drugs. When pain cannot be controlled by these measures and is resulting in loss of condition, drug therapy will be necessary but should be kept to a minimum. With severe lamenesses, neurectomy (cutting the nerve supply to the area) or a long-term nerve block may be preferable to heavy use of systemic drugs. Alcohol blocks involve the injection of strong alcohol solutions around the nerve and last for several months.

Broodmare Nutrition

The other major pregnancy-related problems are those related to nutrition. These include generalized loss of condition, anemia, and bone problems.

As the horse ages, there may be a decreased efficiency of the digestive tract. This becomes a significant problem when the mare must deal with the other demands specific to pregnancy—i.e., greater need for total calories but increasing abdominal distention that causes discomfort and often decreased appetite. The diet of the aged pregnant mare should be very carefully planned to maximize the calorie content of the feeds while still keeping sufficient fiber to aid normal digestion. This is covered in detail in Chapter 3, "Feeding the Older Horse."

The breeding season and lactation period also have specific caloric requirements. It is a common myth (or half-truth) that fat mares are harder to get in foal. The fact is that research has shown that animals that are on a rising plane of nutrition are the easiest to breed. A rising plane of nutrition refers to a high-quality diet and a gradual weight gain. Very fat or very thin mares are both more difficult to breed. Therefore, nutritional planning for the broodmare should begin before she is even taken to the breeding shed.

If the mare has been getting the usual subsistence diet of "barren mare hay" (a euphemism for the worst possible hay), she will require several weeks of a good diet before she is likely to conceive. The feed chosen should be the same that will be used throughout pregnancy and lactation. The mare should be gradually brought up to the level it is anticipated she will need for the first half of pregnancy. A slow weight gain is desirable at this time and even in the early parts of pregnancy as it can be expected that the aged mare will develop problems during her pregnancy that prevent adequate intake of calories in the later stages; this small weight gain acts as an insurance policy against her losing too much condition. While extreme obesity should be avoided early in the breeding season and pregnancy, calorie-counting has absolutely no place in the management of the aged broodmare.

Finally, during lactation, the calorie requirements are about twice what they are for the breeding season and first half to two-thirds of the pregnancy. In addition, if the mare had problems during the pregnancy she may have lost a considerable amount of condition, placing her in a yet more precarious position. It is best to plan increases in feed so that the mare is being offered the amount of feed she will require to maintain lactation by the time she reaches the last three to four weeks of pregnancy. She probably won't always eat this much, but by trying to keep her just a little bit ahead of time on anticipated calorie needs you should be able to avoid trying to make a large jump when it is discovered after foaling that the mare is in poor condition.

In addition to the need for increased calories to nourish herself and the growing foal, the mare requires additional vitamins and minerals during pregnancy. The greatest demands are placed on B vitamins, calcium, phosphorus, copper, and iron—the key elements in the formation of blood (prevention of anemia) and formation and maintenance of normal bones and teeth.

During pregnancy, the blood volume increases and the mare will need to manufacture more red blood cells to meet this requirement. In addition, she must supply all the elements that the developing foal needs to make his own red blood cells. This places a large drain on the stores of iron in the body and also calls for adequate amounts of B-12, folate (another B vitamin), and copper. The pregnant mare's diet will usually contain adequate amounts of these elements themselves or, in the case of the B vitamins, adequate nutrition that the microorganisms of the intestine can manufacture them. However, for this system to operate smoothly, the mare must eat regularly and well and have a perfectly normal digestive tract. Also, since repeated pregnancies drain iron stores, it is at least possible that an aged mare could become anemic in the face of a good diet and healthy appetite.

The best course is to have the mare's hemoglobin and hematocrit checked prior to breeding or in early pregnancy and again in the last trimester. The testing need only be a hematocrit to measure the percentage of red blood cells in the blood and a hemoglobin level to measure the amount of iron in the red blood cells. These tests are fairly inexpensive, but they are very important. They can tell you if the mare is anemic and also help to determine what elements she is lacking. If an anemia is detected, further tests may be recommended to pinpoint the exact deficiency involved. Supplementation may then be given in the feed or by injection, depending on the individual case and the likelihood of any gastrointestinal disturbance contributing to the picture.

Calcium and phosphorus are probably the most neglected components of a pregnant mare's diet, yet deficiencies of these elements result in bone and joint deformities in the foal and weakening of the bones and joints of the mare (osteoporosis). In a retrospective study of metabolic bone disease (osteochondrosis dessicans) in foals, it was found that farms with the lowest incidence fed a diet containing 1.2 percent calcium while the greatest incidence was found on a farm feeding 0.2 percent calcium diets, indicating a direct link between calcium intake and the incidence of metabolic bone disease in foals. In the mare, a deficiency in the diet results in her body trying to make up the difference by dissolving her bones to provide the needed calcium and phosphorus for the foal. With each pregnancy she loses more and more bone until joints begin to lose their support and fractures appear virtually anywhere—most commonly in areas already weakened by an arthritic process, such as the navicular bone.

The common diets fed to horses are usually borderline in the total amount of calcium or phosphorus, depending upon the ration. The all-time favorite of timothy hay and oats has an excellent ratio of calcium to phosphorus but falls a little short on the total amounts. (See discussion in Chapter 3, "Feeding the Older Horse," for details on the calcium to phosphorus ratio.) Young adult horses, however, seem to tolerate this borderline status without any clinically obvious problems.

There are many calcium/phosphorus supplements available, and your

Table 7

Calcium and Phosphorus Requirements in Pregnancy and Lactation

Estimated Calcium Requirement (g/day)
A. Maintenance: Ca = 0.04 BW
B. Pregnant Mares (9 to 11 months)
$$Ca = 1.90 \times Mcal \ of \ DE/day$$

Estimated Phosphorus Requirement (g/day)
A. Maintenance: P = 0.028 BW
B. Pregnant Mares (9 to 11 months)
$$P = 1.41 \times Mcal \ of \ DE/day$$

Key:
g/day = grams per day	Mcal = megacalories
Ca = calcium	DE/day = digestible energy per day
BW = body weight	P = phosphorus

veterinarian will recommend one that best suits your mare's situation and diet. It is critical that the owner of an aged broodmare attend to these calcium and phosphorus needs at all times as limb deformities in foals and osteoporosis in the mare are difficult if not impossible to reverse after the fact.

The newest information regarding pregnancy and nutrition relates to the roles of zinc and copper in preventing metabolic bone disease. The same study mentioned above recommends that levels of 90 mg/kg of zinc be fed during pregnancy to decrease the chances of metabolic bone disease. This is greater than twice what the current NRC (National Research Council) suggests. However, given that zinc is extremely well tolerated at levels of up to even 500 mg/kg/day and that older horses have decreased efficiency of absorption, I would recommend feeding the higher level of zinc to a pregnant mare. A supplemental source of zinc will be required. Consult your veterinarian or an equine nutritionist for advice.

With copper, the recommended level to prevent metabolic bone disease (30 to 50 mg/kg) is three to five times that listed as appropriate in the NRC guidelines. Again, however, the higher level is safe. Also to be strongly considered here is that older mares commonly have low serum levels of copper and that low serum copper is believed to be associated with another problem of pregnancy, ruptured ovarian artery. For these reasons, again I recommend supplementing mares up to the higher level of copper intake.

Buying a Broodmare at Auction

Many broodmares are sold at auction where the information available is sketchy at best, and you will not be able to have the benefit of a complete examination. In these cases, it is necessary to try to read between the lines of a mare's breeding history.

There are many possible reasons why a mare would fail to conceive in any given year. These would include postpartum infection or foaling trauma on the mare's side but also improper timing of breedings or poor semen quality—causes that have nothing to do with her fertility per se. I cannot give hard and fast guidelines here, but a rule of thumb would be that even a normal mare could have a "failure" rate of 10 to 25 percent (i.e., barren an average of one to two and one-half years out of ten, assuming she was bred every year).

However, you should check the foaling dates. A trend to steadily later foaling dates, leading up to a barren year, could indicate that the mare is difficult to breed and/or prone to infections that must be treated before she can be bred back. That is, if she consistently needs two or more cycles to conceive, foalings will get progressively later until she must miss a year. Also, caution is always advisable if the mare previously had a 100 percent conception rate but failed to conceive for one or more years immediately prior to her sale. While it may simply be that this is normal but the present owner is unwilling to invest another season of maintenance in an aged mare, it may indicate that she has developed a problem. Owners are aware that this looks bad in a sales catalog and will usually try to explain somewhat in an "Owner's Statement" at the bottom of the page.

Many sales catalogs do not specify if a mare was bred or not in any year she failed to conceive. A listing of "open" means only that she was not carrying a foal, not that she was not bred. "Barren" usually means that she was bred but did not conceive or lost the foal early in the pregnancy; however, this use of the term is by no means universal and this listing may also mean that she was not bred. Always attempt to get a definition of the terminology used from the sales company if possible.

To simplify this discussion, you will want to evaluate a mare's breeding record in two ways. First of all, look at her lifetime breeding history. She should fall within the 10 to 25 percent failure rate for all the years she was actually bred. If you cannot determine whether or not she was bred any given year, check the foaling date from the preceding year. If it was early and her only use was as a broodmare, you must assume she was bred but did not conceive (or lost the foal) until proven otherwise. If her failure rate was above 25 percent, a clustering of the "open" or "barren" years probably represents some fertility problem at that time.

The second step is to evaluate the recent reproductive history, that is, the last four years. Ideally, you want a mare that had a foal the preceding year and is in foal at the time of the sale. Failing this, look for a mare who foaled the preceding year and is not bred back but has an owner's statement explaining why. If there is no owner's statement, there may be a recent problem that prompted this sale. This purchase would be a gamble; however, the foaling the previous year and recent onset of difficulty may mean it is something you can deal with successfully. If the mare did not have a foal the preceding year, the likelihood of there being a serious problem is higher and increases with each additional preceding year she did not foal. This is particularly true if her reproductive history prior to the last four years was normal.

If it cannot be determined whether or not she was bred, you probably should not buy this mare. However, if the history shows that she did conceive but lost the foal early in the pregnancy there is at least a chance that the problem may be treatable. Such early losses may be related to infection secondary to poor conformation (amenable to surgery), or to placental or uterine abnormalities that would respond to administration of progesterone injections during the critical months. However, they could also be related to uterine scarring that will not respond to any measures. The purchase would be a gamble but perhaps one well worth taking if the price is right. Remember too that there is no reason to typecast these ladies. If the mare is otherwise healthy and sound there is no reason why she could not change careers and be resold (or kept) as a riding or driving horse after some retraining.

To summarize then, mares can produce foals well into their teens. Their experience in raising foals, known reproductive history, and often reasonable price makes such mares a very good choice for the first-time breeder, and many mares can also double as a family horse.

However, increasing age does result in an increased risk of fertility problems, greater number of risks associated with pregnancy, and special nutritional requirements. Fortunately, modern veterinary medicine has much to offer in the diagnosis of problems and management of the special requirements of the aged broodmare. By working closely with your veterinarian it will be possible to maximize the reproductive efficiency and general health of the aged broodmare.

THE AGED BREEDING STALLION

Compared to mares, the breeding stallion has relatively few problems associated with age and/or time that refer specifically to his reproductive capacity. In fact, it is not at all unusual to hear of stallions performing quite adequately well into their twenties.

Breeding can be affected by nonspecific problems such as advancing arthritis, particularly if the disease involves extensive changes in the hindlegs and/or pelvis or spine that causes pain when the stallion must mount a mare. These studs may reach the point where they refuse to mount the mare and/or develop a syndrome of general poor condition and decreased sperm numbers or quality secondary to the stress of chronic pain.

Cardiovascular System Problems

Cardiovascular system problems involving the heart, its valves, or the major vessels appear with some degree of frequency in aged breeding stallions. This is probably primarily related to the fact that they commonly achieve such an advanced age and/or are allowed to live out their normal lifespans since they continue to perform a useful function. While these difficulties do not have any effect upon reproductive performance per se, it is advisable to remember that the likelihood of a significant circulatory problem increases with age and to avoid unusual exercise or stress with older horses. One stress that cannot be controlled is the excitement of breeding; in fact, it is fairly common for such stallions to die during the act of breeding.

Declining Sperm Counts and Quality

Declines in sperm numbers and/or quality can be expected as a natural result of aging, but this rarely reaches the point where breeding must stop altogether. The sperm counts and quality should be checked by the veterinarian before the start of each breeding season and at intervals into the season so that the proper adjustments in bookings of mares can be planned. The magnitude of this problem is greatly reduced when the modern technology of semen extenders and methods for storing semen are employed to make the most of each ejaculate.

Declining Reproductive Efficiency

Declining reproductive efficiency is related to multiple changes in the endocrine balance with aging, and injudicious use of male hormones is not advisable, nor is it likely to prove effective. In selected cases, however, it may be found that the problem is acutely linked to a drop in thyroid hormone levels, usually associated with some intercurrent nonspecific stress such as a prolonged illness or serious injury. In these cases, the imbalance is caused by factors operating above and beyond those to be expected from aging, and the veterinarian may recommend a temporary and strictly monitored course of supplementation to aid recovery.

Managing the Aged Breeding Stallion

The key areas of management of the aged breeding stallion are exercise and diet. Reproductive activity does, as indicated above, place a considerable stress on the cardiovascular system but does very little to maintain muscle tone and joint/tendon flexibility and strength. The naturally aggressive nature of stallions, together with special requirements for isolation and extremely strong and high fencing during turnout, often results in their not getting the proper amount of exercise. Stallions are naturally more exuberant, alert, playful, and strong than mares or geldings, but they are not naturally mean. It is important they be handled by someone who is comfortable with stallions and does not resort to confining them to their stall to avoid confrontations or overreact to their normal behavior with fear and excessive force.

A stallion who has been improperly handled and kept confined for a number of years can develop many dangerous vices such as biting, striking, kicking, and charging any human in range. However, even these patterns can be changed with proper handling, and every effort should be made to re-educate such horses so that they can be safely exercised to maintain some degree of musculoskeletal fitness and to prevent any chronic arthritic problems from degenerating into permanent pain and stiffness.

Generally speaking, fifteen to twenty minutes per day of free turnout, driving, longeing, or riding is adequate for the breeding stallion. Heavier exercise schedules are not harmful (unless extremely stressful) as long as measures are made to provide dietary increases to meet the higher energy demands.

Since most stallions are maintained at minimum exercise levels, feeding them involves a very delicate balance of providing high-quality feed needed for top reproductive performance without causing excessive weight gain or digestive disturbances. The National Research Council recommends that breeding stallions be fed a diet similar to that given to mares in the last third of pregnancy: specifically, 0.75 pounds to 1.5 pounds of 50 percent legume hay per 100 pounds per day with an equal amount of grain. Recommended grain mixtures include:

1. Oats, 55%; Wheat, 20%; Wheat bran, 20%; Soybean meal, 5%
2. Corn, 35%; Oats, 35%; Wheat, 15%; Wheat bran, 15%
3. Oats alone

The ration of oats alone is most appropriate for stallions who tend to gain weight on even the minimal amounts of recommended feed and/or are not being used heavily. This diet is also lower in protein, and the stallion getting only oats should be fed a very good quality of hay or be given soybean meal substituted for 5 percent of his oat ration. In addition, salt should be offered free choice at all times and he should receive whatever level of additional calcium and phosphorus supplementation is needed for the specific diet fed, as detailed elsewhere.

PART III

The Later Years

14

A Child's Best Friend

There's a magic in children and horses. Older horses, with the patience and kindness acquired through years of association with people, are the perfect choice for children.

To all aged horses, here is a special thank-you from all the generations you have lovingly cared for, who will return the favor now, in your declining years.

Michelle Hoffman, age nine, of Davis, California, is happy to tell anyone about her horse, "Rocky Road," a 23-year-old gelding. She started showing on "Rocky" at the age of five and got a second-place ribbon at their first small show. At the age of six she received her first blue ribbon, although, as Michelle puts it, "Now that I think about it, it was Rock's ribbon because I was six years old and I could barely stay on a horse.... He followed tiny kicks (from her) and ... voice commands." Michelle and "Rocky" continue to enjoy many activities together, and she is so proud of her horse she lists her address as "Rocky Road Ranch."

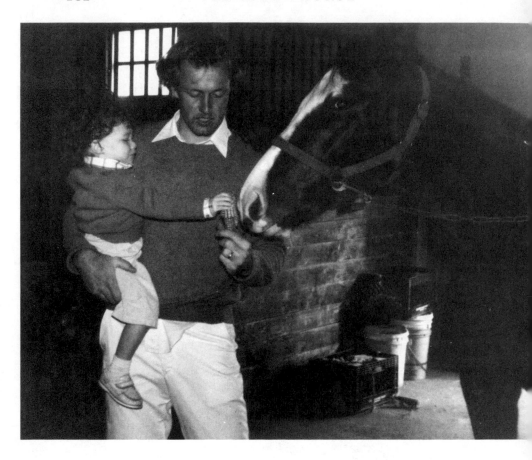

Author's husband, Andy, with 23-month-old daughter, Erica, and a friend, "Patches."

Lisa Goldrick has owned her pony "Rocket J. Squirrel" for fifteen years and guesses his present age to be close to her own, late twenties. When she outgrew him he served her for many years as a driving Pony. His most recent career change is to the role of companion and teacher to Lisa's recently acquired yearling Saddlebred filly, "Once a Gypsy," and he is shown here ponying "Once a Gypsy" with Lisa. (Photograph by CARYN.)

Perhaps the best example of the bond between child and older horse is the joy to be found in riding centers for the handicapped, such as the Shenandoah Valley Special Riding Program of Port Republic, Virginia. The horses and ponies were all donations, and they have continued to lead useful and valued lives in their new capacity.

"Princess." Rider: Anne Bailey. Volunteer: Teresa Townsend.

"Princess," 21-year-old Quarter Horse/Arabian. Rider: Jamie Ratatczak. Volunteer: Sherry Miller.

"Pooky," 16-year-old Shetland. Rider: Christopher Eby. Volunteers: Julie Cross and Julie Layman.

Not all beginners are children! "Something Special," 16, is a Thoroughbred retired from a racing career and now teaching her amateur-owner Mary Ann Donahue of Hamilton, Massachusetts, the ropes about Combined Training. Photograph by V.J. Zabek.

15

The Last Days: Retirement and Turnout

*I*t's a lovely image—horses enjoying a well-earned retirement, living out their days in a thick, green pasture with stately trees and a sparkling brook. In reality, it takes a good deal of planning, supervision, and attention to detail to make the life of an older horse on turnout as pleasant as the expectation.

Retirement for some horses means no greater change in their life than never being tacked up again. They still spend at least a portion of every day in a stall and are turned out regularly in a familiar paddock or small field, with or without familiar companions. For others the major change is relegation to life outside unless weather conditions are extreme but still on a familiar pasture and with familiar companions. The third group are horses whose owners either send them to a farm that offers retirement to pasture at very low prices or "loan" them to families where they are used only rarely to entertain the children and otherwise spend their days turned out under a wide variety of possible conditions. Each of these situations will require certain modifications to management techniques. The following discussion is designed to provide information applicable to the horse shipped to a retirement farm, kept at home, or anything in between but centers on the horse who will be experiencing a change in environment and turnout with a herd of other, often strange horses, as this requires the most planning and revision of normal routines.

All the ingredients for turnout—shade, good pasture, and a water source.

HOME ON THE RANGE

The physical conditions of a turnout facility are obviously central to success. Accidents can happen at any time, even to the horse who is only out for an hour or so daily, by himself, and right outside his owner's window. The conditions of the turnout assume critical importance, however, for the horse who spends all his time outdoors, largely unsupervised. Even a location that looks extremely inviting on first view must stand up to a careful inspection. A primary (and often overlooked) consideration is safety, particularly if the horse will not be checked on a daily basis.

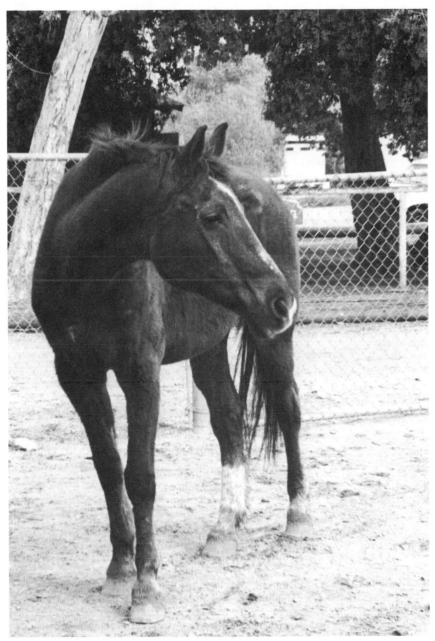

Chain link fencing, with smooth rounded metal supports and tops, is a very durable and safe approach. Shown here in the comfort of his "loafing area" is "Sam," a 30-year-old gelding owned by Anita Sohus, of LaCanada, California.

Fencing

A logical place to start is with the fencing. Do not assume that older horses will not attempt to break out. Even retirees may be smitten with wanderlust, particularly if they are located in close proximity to an appealing food source such as a field of corn or grassy areas that will not deteriorate under the stress of continued grazing late in the year.

Accidents can also occur if fights break out, if the horses are chased by dogs, if they are spooked by a motorcycle, or even when they lean over the fencing to get at the grass that usually is really greener on the other side of the fence for most of the year!

Fencing must be solid and in good repair, with no weak areas to tempt escape. It should be carefully inspected for splintered wood, protruding nails, or areas patched together with rope or wire. You should also consider the type of fencing used. Wire, barbed or otherwise, should be avoided. Even a horse who is accustomed to wire fencing would be safer in an area enclosed by another fencing as most fence-related injuries occur during a moment of panic when the horse could not care less whether he is trying to get through wire or stone. Wire is particularly dangerous because it can trap a horse and cause considerable damage if he struggles to free himself. If wire must be used, it should be checked at regular intervals to guarantee it is tight and all supports firm and upright. Sagging fencelines may invite the horse to experiment with its stability. When introducing a horse to wire fencing for the first time, it may be helpful to attach rags or some other highly visible object to the top strand just to be certain he sees it. This, however, has little value for horses who know about wire and will not stop any horse from testing the fence. If the choice is between barbed and electrified wire, the electrified is probably the best choice as it will earn the horse's respect without damaging him (even if he should become tangled up in it) as severely in an accident.

The safest fencing is probably a chain link type; however, it is seldom used because of its prohibitively high cost. Meshed wire fencing sometimes works if the supporting frame and posts are especially solid, but it requires very careful maintenance. The ever-popular post and rail can work well when properly maintained; however, it does not stand up for very long to horses that lean on the fence line. Rubber fencing, used in some areas, is considered desirable from the view of preventing injuries. However, many horses tend to chew on it, particularly as it begins to unravel, and the resultant intestinal impaction almost inevitably requires surgery. Other possibilities include pipe or plank fencing, which tend to offer good long-term strength, a key consideration, particularly when posts are seated in cement.

Solid fencing is an investment in safety. Shown is "Henry," a 23-year-old owned by Leslie Young of Tenafly, New Jersey.

Fence chewing is a fact of life with most horses, most notably during the winter months. The chain-link and pipe fences eliminate this problem, although the horse may then turn to attacking trees. Chemical treatment of wood fences may discourage this behavior temporarily. In any event, chewing damage should be looked for regularly and worn areas replaced to decrease the chance of injury to the mouth or gastrointestinal tract from wood splinters.

Feeding

Next on a safety checklist are the arrangements for feeding. If the horse is only turned out part of the day, it is common and advisable practice to feed him in his stall. This makes it easier to bring him in, avoids wasted feed, and is generally more convenient. Even hay should be fed indoors unless the turnout area is totally devoid of grass (as in winter).

If the horse is on constant turnout, but alone or with only one or two other horses, he can be fed in much the same way as when he was stabled, with buckets hung on the fence or in the shed and firmly secured to avoid spillage or the chance of the horse pulling them down and catching a foot. Recommendations noted later for maintaining the buckets and surrounding area should be followed for single horses or small groups as well as for a larger herd.

Horses usually adjust well to group feeding once a pecking order has been established. Fighting can be minimized by placing out an extra bucket of feed or extra pile of hay. This is a good idea even if grain and hay are offered from a central trough and large hay rack. It ensures that horses chased away from feeding areas will have another source and actually minimizes such competitiveness.

Areas used for feeding should be well drained as parasite larvae thrive in moisture. Because the location for grain feedings is usually constant, e.g., a large trough or buckets hung on a fence line, this high traffic area tends to accumulate manure. It is best, therefore, to feed the hay at several different locations in the field to minimize parasite contamination on the ground. Ideally, hay should be fed from a high bunker. Such a bunker will pay for itself quickly in hay otherwise lost to mud and trampling. Don't be surprised though if horses prefer to remove the hay to ground level before eating it.

All central feeding areas should be regularly scraped of manure (not simply harrowed) and even limed as accumulated feces can provide a local microenvironment of sufficient heat and moisture to support parasites even in the middle of winter.

Horses on turnout have the same salt requirements as stabled horses. The best arrangement is to place the large 25- to 50-pound blocks of salt close to, but not directly in, feeding areas or near the water supply. These will last quite a long time, even when fully exposed to the weather, and work far better than the smaller blocks that horses can move around.

Water Supply

An adequate supply of fresh water can be a real problem for horses on turnout. One solution is to have a pond. Ponds are attractive as well as functional. Be sure that pond banks are gradual and offer solid footing for safety and ease of access. Stream-fed ponds usually have satisfactory water quality. Under certain conditions, however, algae growth may be a problem. Of particular concern is blue-green algae accumulation along banks as this can result in poisoning. Algae can also build up in slow-moving streams. Contact your extension agent for advice on algae-preventative treatments, such as copper sulfate, and be sure to mention the water source is used for horses.

Even if water is provided from a pond or stream, an alternate method of watering should be available should this source dry up, become unsuitable, or freeze over.

Ponds used as a water source should have low or no banks and a level access.

Water may be given in bathtubs, metal troughs, or individual buckets. If large community tubs are used, they should be of sufficient size to hold a minimum of five gallons per horse and should be easy to drain for cleaning. Tubs should be checked and filled at least twice daily. They should also be cleaned daily by scrubbing the insides with a stiff brush and then draining out the water. This is not a problem with bathtubs or other receptacles that have a bottom drain. If the container has to be tipped to drain it, only fill it with approximately as much water as will be consumed in a day's time. (You should seriously consider replacing any water tub that cannot be easily cleaned.)

Among the problems associated with such watering arrangements is ice formation. Floating heaters may solve this, and pumps that drain after use to keep water below the freeze line will save hauling in water. Experience has shown, however, that no ice-proofing method is perfect, and contingency plans for bringing in water should allow for the worst possible conditions. Horses will not and cannot get enough water from eating snow.

Safety

As a final safety check, the entire area should be inspected for holes, discarded wire, glass, and other foreign items such as nails or pieces of metal. Animals should never be placed on a field where dumping has been made in the past. What appears to be a dense growth of brush or ground cover may hide layer upon layer of trash that can easily collapse under a horse's weight. If the field borders on a road, periodic checks will have to be made to pick up bottles and cans from littering. It is also wise to inspect for thistles, cockleburs, and similar plants that can cause breaks in the skin or become tangled in manes and tails.

To summarize, it is wise to adopt an "if-it-can-go-wrong-it-will" attitude where the comfort and safety of horses on pasture is concerned. It is impossible to be too cautious, particularly when your horse will spend long periods without supervision.

Shelter

The question of shelter is frequently raised when horses are turned out. Just as the lush green grass gives way to parched earth and snow, so the image of sunny days and balmy, starlit nights is replaced by a wide variety of unpleasant weather conditions.

If the horse is out only part of the day and with someone around to bring him in and care for him if the weather turns bad, no outside shelter is needed. (A horse that is turned out for a few hours and spends the whole

A housing and turn-out combination that is convenient for owner and horse is a barn with stalls designed to open out into a turn-out area. Photograph courtesy of Lester Building Systems, Lester Prairie, Minnesota.

Treated plank fencing lasts a long time and is also a very safe fencing choice. Photograph courtesy of Lester Building Systems, Lester Prairie, Minnesota.

Roomy, sturdy, three-sided turnout shed with feeding trough running the length of the far wall and overhead hay rack. The floor is covered in sand for good drainage and ease of cleaning. Note also the board fencing and the arrangement with aisles between paddocks.

time in a shed because the weather is so poor may as well be in his stall.) The only precaution would be the common-sense measure of putting him out during the nicest part of the day (midday in winter, evening in summer).

When a shelter is needed for horses on constant turnout, a three-sided shed, with the back facing the direction from which most severe storms originate, is the best choice for field shelter. The best direction to face the shed is influenced by the local weather patterns and also any geographical/topographical factors such as sheltering or protecting stands of trees, hills, or mountain ranges. The builder or contractor, if familiar with houses, barns, and sheds, can help to determine how to place the facility, and the local weather bureau can tell you from which direction most severe storms originate.

The shed should be large enough to house all animals easily (ideally, twelve square feet per horse would be a good guide) and be placed on high ground with the floor sloping slightly outward to aid cleaning and prevent water accumulation. Walls should be smooth and free of nails or hooks. If hay racks are to be placed in the shed, they must be high enough to prevent a horse from catching a leg in them (although height alone is not a sufficient safeguard against trapped limbs if a horse rears). Slats should either be too narrow to admit a foot (or knee) or sufficiently wide to allow it to easily pull through.

The flooring should be firmly packed as this will be a high traffic area if used for feeding. High traffic of course will also mean the shed will need mucking out regularly.

Finally, try to locate the shed in an area regularly frequented as the horse will probably not go out of his way to seek shelter. In fact, you may often make the maddening discovery that the horses prefer to turn their rumps to the storm but remain outside! With this in mind, it is a good practice to at least occasionally use the shed for feeding if you do not already do so as this results in the horses frequenting it more often and will make it easier to lead them to shelter if need be. If your horse's pasture is extremely large and/or if there is no barn close by, it is wise to consider placing a fence around the shed to create a small paddock that can be used when dewormings, trimmings, or other procedures are necessary. Entry and exit should be through one, or preferably two, very large gates, such as cattle gates, which can be secured open when the paddock is not needed.

SUPERVISION ON TURNOUT

Even when the greatest care has been taken with the safety and comfort of a horse's new surroundings, he should not simply be turned loose and forgotten except for routine veterinary or blacksmith visits. Although accidents can happen anytime and anywhere, constant observation is not likely to prevent them, and prevention in the form of the noted safety measures is the best approach.

The ideal system is one that allows for daily inspection. If the horses are being fed or watered, that is obviously the time to check them. If turnout is only for part of the day, make a habit of checking for cuts, swellings, loose shoes, and damaged blankets or halter when the horse comes in and watch him for a few minutes in the stall to be sure he is behaving normally and eating well.

A head count is a good place to start, but it is not enough simply to note all are accounted for. The caretaker should be alert to the general attitude of the horse—is he unusually depressed or anxious?—and should quickly observe for other signs of distress, such as standing off alone, rapid respirations, sweating (or sweat dried on the coat), or flared nostrils. The caretaker should also inspect the horse from the front, back, and both sides and watch him walk or trot a few steps. The knowledgeable observer can perform the examinations in a minute or two and will

This attractive little shed is designed like a home-away-from-home with all the conveniences of a stall. Hay is fed in a small rack over the grain bowls; salt in a flat, corner-mounted container; and water from a bucket on the floor. The "living space" is adjoined by a small storage area for hay and grain.

This simple but well-designed barn conveniently opens out into the paddock, allowing horses freedom and constant access to protection from the elements, a water source, and dry, clean hay. Photograph courtesy of Lester Building Systems, Lester Prairie, Minnesota.

use his or her general experience, plus a familiarity with the horse's individual patterns and preferences, to detect problems early.

Any horse acting or even looking suspiciously abnormal should be caught and examined more closely. It may simply be he was dozing, but extra caution is always in order since the horse will be on his own until the next check. If still in doubt after catching the horse, you should recheck him in an hour or so and/or confine him.

Deworming, trimming, and tooth-floating visits should also be used as opportunities for a close inspection. Pay particular attention to the ears, eyes, mouth, belly, axillae (armpits), and bottoms of the feet as injuries or other problems in these areas could easily be missed on the routine superficial examinations.

ROUTINE HEALTH CARE ON PASTURE

With regard to deworming and other maintenance health care, it should go without saying that retirement should not signal any laxity. If anything, the special needs of older horses often dictate a more rigidly observed schedule of prophylaxis.

Deworming

Deworming needs alter with age and life on pasture. Older horses, as discussed in detail in Chapter 2, are less tolerant of any insult to the digestive tract. Burdens that were handled with apparent ease earlier in adulthood may now contribute to significant problems with normal contraction patterns in the intestine that result in spasmodic colic or impaction. Such problems can usually be treated very successfully with nonsurgical methods—but only when diagnosed early. Early signs of trouble include mild depression, decreased manure production, and depressed food and water consumption—any or all of which are very difficult to detect under field conditions. The result can be a delay that results in more difficulty with treatment, possibly even necessitating surgery.

Also, increasing age often results in a decrease in the ability to fight parasite infestations. The loss in local immunity in the intestines often results in patterns of parasitism that are more typical of young foals—for example, large numbers of roundworms. This dictates a change in drugs used for deworming.

Finally, age inevitably means the horse has accumulated some degree of permanent damage from a lifetime of parasite exposure. The most significant change usually involves the arteries that feed the intestines and is a result of repeated migrations of immature bloodworms—the large strongyles. The horse that has been poised on the edge of a clinical problem for years can easily become affected under pasture conditions. The end result is development of a chronic problem with refractory colic and/or life-threatening interruption of blood flow to the intestine.

When a horse makes the move from life in a stall to turnout it is logical to assume he will have a different level of exposure to parasites. Many people assume parasite numbers will decreased in the expanse of a pasture. In fact, exposure is often higher as manure from many horses accumulates in high-traffic areas such as along fence lines, at watering or feeding areas, and even in certain spots out in the field where the grass is most tasty. This problem alone will probably mean dewormings should be more frequent than for stabled horses. Even a horse turned out alone or in a small group will have a different exposure level unless his paddock is cleaned as regularly and as well as his stall. If he is grazing while turned out, or receiving hay outside in the winter, he should also be put on the more intensive deworming schedule. (Regular scraping of these areas will greatly decrease the exposure but is not sufficient protection.)

Another factor to consider in planning deworming for horses on pasture is a seasonal variation in egg counts. Bots of course are limited to the summer months when the botflies are active. Research also suggests that egg-laying in other species is more active in the late spring and early summer months. Thus, while stabled horses are at greatest risk when passing through a sale barn, breeding farm, show stabling, or anywhere the turnover of horses is high, the retirees have a seasonal pattern to the periods most dangerous for parasite infestation. This calls for concentration of deworming immediately before and during periods of greatest egg-laying activity.

Table 8 is a suggested rotational deworming schedule for horses on year-round turnout. It takes into consideration the seasonal high-risk period and the older horse's susceptibility to a wider range of parasites than younger adult horses, while avoiding resistance problems. The major points include a concentration of deworming in the spring months, provisions for the possibility of significant roundworm or strongyloides infestations, avoidance of resistance problems with use of similar drugs, and a double deworming schedule for bots that is designed to eliminate infection acquired early and late in the season. Adjustments may be made as needed for geographical and/or climactic differences. That is, as the difference between the seasons narrows, seasonal differences in egg-laying are minimized.

As mentioned in Chapter 2, the rotational deworming schedule can be greatly simplified by substitution of ivermectin for all of the drugs listed in Table 8. Also, daily deworming with low dose pyrantel pamoate, as detailed in Chapter 2, would probably be the deworming program of

Table 8

Suggested Rotational Deworming Schedule for Horses on Pasture

Time	Suggested Agents
April 1st	Benzimidazole family (pick one): thiabendazole, mebendazole, cambendazole, fenbendazole, oxfendazole, and oxibendazole
Mid-May	Pyrantel pamoate or morantel tartrate
End of June	Ivermectin
September 1st	Dichlorvos, trichlorfon, ivermectin, or piperzaine/carbon disulfide
January 1st	Dichlorvos, trichlorfon, ivermectin, or piperazine/carbon disulfide

(See Chapter 2 for more details on deworming agents)

choice for horses on pasture. However, unless the horse is turned out alone, or arrangements have been made to segregate horses during feeding, it may not be practical for turnout conditions (i.e., there would be no way to guarantee each horse is getting the proper daily dose).

As a final note on parasite control when using any program other than daily pyrantel pamoate, fecal examinations for egg counts should be done before adding a new horse to the group and after that horse's first deworming. The first test will aid in detecting any large parasite burdens that may require special attention. The second examination will uncover any lesser burdens that could have been masked on the previous fecal examination by another, dominant population of worms.

A third fecal examination should also be done at four to six months after the horse is added to the herd. This will uncover any heavy bloodworm burden that may have been in the immature, non-egg-laying stage on earlier testing.

The fecal examination may seem to be an unnecessary expense and bother when a good deworming program is observed. However, the goal of proper parasite management must be to minimize exposure, rather than to repeatedly, albeit effectively, treat large burdens. Deworming schedules are the same for either philosophy. The difference lies in minimizing the potential damage done by stages of worms unaffected by routine dewormings, particularly immature bloodworms that do their most significant damage—to the arteries of the intestines—while in immature stages.

Vaccination

Some alterations in vaccination schedules are also indicated for older horses on pasture. Infectious diseases and their consequences are discussed in detail in Chapter 2. Unless you are 100 percent certain your horse will never be moved or exposed to a new horse, he should have the same protection against influenza, rhinopneumonitis, and possibly strangles as any other older horse. His risk of exposure may indeed be less but the possible consequences are too severe to try to cut corners here. Risk for encephalitis is just as great as for more active horses since this disease is spread by an insect. Rabies is a must, as is Potomac horse fever in appropriate areas. The tetanus vaccination as well will remain vital in his preventive health-care program.

The horse retired on pasture is at even greater danger from tetanus due to the increased possibility of injuries that will possibly be unattended and/or undetected for a longer period. Tetanus, remember, thrives best in deep puncture wounds where the flesh at the skin surface may swell and close over the deeper hole. This can be very difficult to detect on cursory inspections, particularly if bleeding was slight.

If your horse is to be shipped to a facility where he will be retired to pasture with other horses, and it is known that the group is often added to, it is best to have him vaccinated for influenza and rhinopneumonitis two weeks prior to the anticipated shipping date. This will provide for strong and immediately effective protection when he arrives. Tetanus vaccination should also be done at this time unless he was recently vaccinated. If spring is approaching, you might also wish to give the encephalitis series at this time. After this initial series of vaccinations, boosters can be scheduled as you would for a stabled horse. He should also have a Coggins test, as many facilities require a current (within six months) negative test for all incoming horses.

Lyme Disease

Lyme disease is a problem caused by the organism *Borrelia burgdorferi,* which is transmitted by tick bites. Obviously, horses kept outdoors for prolonged periods are at the greatest risk. Signs at the time of the bite are minimal, including local irritation and a fever. However, the organism becomes seated in the joints where it causes joint swelling and a shifting lameness.

Lyme disease can be treated, but only if it is diagnosed. It is easy to dismiss periods of lameness as due to changes in the ground, flare-ups of old arthritis problems, etc. The important thing is to be aware that Lyme disease is a possibility. Suspect it if the horse shows signs of lameness and joint swelling during or after tick season.

If possible, a daily check for ticks is a wise practice. They are most likely to be found in the long hairs of the fetlock, under the mane, or in the tail hairs. Keeping the hair of the fetlock trimmed short and the mane roached will decrease the likelihood of tick bite.

Foot Care

Another key element in routine health care is foot care. While usually a horse will require a minimum of attention, you will not be able to pull his shoes and forget about the feet simply because he is turned out.

At the minimum, the horse will need to be trimmed at six- to eight-week intervals. This prevents the hoof from breaking up and, even more important, allows for inspection and trimming of the frog and sole.

As always, care should be taken to balance the foot and maintain proper alignment with respect to the bones of the lower leg. Special considerations for turnout include:

1. Leaving sufficient layers of sole to provide a good protection
2. Leaving as much heel and toe as possible while maintaining a normal angle to the foot, but not so much that the horse stumbles
3. Taking care to leave enough frog that this structure can perform its normal function as a shock absorber

Many chronic foot problems such as uneven heels, sheared heels, and contracted heels tend to correct themselves when the shoes are pulled and the horse turned out. In fact, if the horse has had a problem with balancing or lameness, the best course is to trim as little as possible and then allow the way the horse wears his feet to dictate how he will be trimmed in the future. Freed of shoes and "corrective" intervention, he will quickly model his feet to conform to the most comfortable and anatomically correct way of moving.

The barefoot horse wearing his feet naturally is ideal. There are a number of horses, however, that will be sore or wear their hoof wall down too quickly without shoes. Even the horse that usually goes barefoot may need extra protection under some conditions, such as an unusually dry summer or icy winter.

If at all possible it is always best to wait at least two weeks before putting shoes back on after the initial turnout. This brief period will help the foot to expand maximally, thus providing a good weight-bearing surface,

Figure 16. Tip Shoes

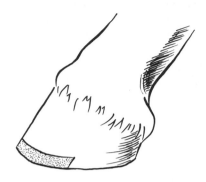

16 a. Bottom View

16 b. Side View
Note how the shoe is set flush
with the hoof wall.

particularly at the heels, and will show how the horse prefers to move
and wear his feet.

If the major problem is breakage of the foot centered at the toe, it may
be possible to apply tip shoes instead of full shoes. This is a half shoe
placed only across the toes (see Figure 16). The wall on either side is
notched and the wall at the shoe site is lowered slightly to allow the tip to
fit flush with the natural hoof on either side. These shoes preserve all
the advantages of going barefoot—i.e., maximal heel expansion, minimal interference with gait—while still preventing excessive breakage.

However, if the horse becomes footsore or has a pre-existing lameness
that required corrective shoeing (e.g., navicular disease), it may not be
possible to keep him comfortable with only tip shoes. Nevertheless, there
are some adjustments that can and should be made. Shoes should be
checked at six-week intervals more often if there is a problem with loos-
ening or loss.

Although there are exceptions, it is often possible to use a lighter shoe
as the soft footing and light exercise result in longer wear. Small horses
may be able to wear an aluminum training plate. If the horse was accustomed to a heavy shoe, such as a field hunter might wear, this change is
as different and welcome as going from army boots to sneakers! Medium
to large horses will not fit in plates (at least not if their feet are trimmed
properly) but can be fitted with handmade aluminum or very lightweight
steel shoes.

These light shoes reduce stress on the leg while maintaining adequate protection. Bars or other special adaptations such as a rolled toe can be added to the lighter shoe if needed. You may find, however, that pads can be eliminated entirely or at least reduced (e.g., from full to rim pad or from plastic to leather).

One drawback to the lighter shoe, particularly plastic shoes, is that the horse may not keep them. This problem will be more likely if there is a tendency for the feet to be brittle or thin-walled, although even horses with good-quality hooves may be troubled with lost shoes. It can be seen under any type of field conditions, wet or dry, rocky or not. On occasion, one or more horses will habitually lose the same shoe. This latter phenomenon is probably an idiosyncrasy of how the blacksmith places his nails. In most other cases, however, lost shoes are caused by conditions that cannot be changed or even identified.

The weight of the shoe per se is not of particular importance in whether or not it will be kept on unless the horse is stepping on a lightweight shoe and bending it. The first step in eliminating this problem is to be certain the shoe fits flush with the heels and quarters. This will not leave much margin for hoof growth, and trimming or resets must be done regularly to avoid corns. If closer fitting of the shoe with subsequent elimination of the horse's chance of pulling it off is not sufficient, larger nails and longer clinches may be tried. The drawback to larger nails is that damage to the hoof will be more extensive if this approach fails and the shoe rips off.

The best solution often proves to be the addition of side clips to the shoe. This requires "hot" shoeing with a forge and is therefore more expensive initially. However, the method more than compensates in saving lost shoes and broken feet.

Feeding

Of all the management concerns for horses on pasture perhaps the most significant is the question of supplemental feeding. The horse who is only turned out for a few hours and kept stabled in bad weather will probably not need any more feed than he was getting before retirement and may even need less, depending upon his prior activity level. However, those turned out year round and expected to get the bulk of their nutrition from pasture are another story. Young spring pastures are undeniably a perfect feed for horses of all ages. One need only look at the good flesh and blooming coats of pastured horses in the spring to see the truth to this. As long as pastures remain in good grass the only other nutrient needs are for fresh water and salt.

Obviously, some sort of regular supplemental feed is essential in the winter and may be needed long before fall if pasture quality falls off. The most obvious sign that more feed is needed is a drop in a horse's weight. There are also earlier, behavioral clues. These include fence chewing, start of (or increase in) attempts to break out, and even personality changes such as irritability and a greater tendency to segregate in a small band.

Many horses will do well on supplementation with hay alone, particularly if mixtures rich in alfalfa are used. The horse will need 1.5 to 1.75 pounds of hay for every 100 pounds of body weight. This ratio will increase in cold weather, in which case it is probably best to start grain feeding as well. It is also important to increase the amount actually fed by how much is trampled on the ground and wasted.

For best results, it is important to feed according to accurate weights, both of the hay and/or grain and of the horse. Invest in a girth tape. These give a fairly accurate estimate of a horse's weight based on the girth measurement. Either weigh several bales of hay or simply ask the supplier for the bale count per ton. If this figure is not available, it is good practice to routinely count the bales as they are being unloaded and divide this into the tonnage yourself.

If the hay contains little or no legumes, the horse should also receive about three-quarters pounds per day of a high-protein supplement such as soybean meal. As the weather turns cold if free choice hay does not maintain weight, supplement grain at one-half pound per day of a mixture of 70 percent oats and 30 percent corn, 70 percent oats and 30 percent barley, or oats alone should be given routinely if only grass hay is fed. This feeding should also be started any time the signs of insufficient feed become evident. If straight alfalfa hay is fed, corn alone can be used in approximately the same amount as the oats or oats mixtures above.

This latter combination may seem unorthodox to some; however, it offers the highest quality protein, excellent energy levels, and often the least expensive option. When feeding corn, however, it is best to avoid corn still on the cob as these can become lodged in the esophagus, causing "choke." It is also vital that corn be stored properly and not be allowed to accumulate in feeding areas where it can develop dangerous mold growths.

Premixed grains can also be used, either commercial or from a local mill that gives a guaranteed analysis in terms of energy and protein. Do not buy a feedmill mixture with an analysis given in terms of amounts of oats, corn, and so forth as the "oats" may well prove to be little more than husks. One drawback to most of these mixtures is that many contain molasses, which is really not necessary and makes the feeds very messy in warm weather. They also have a tendency to freeze into an inedible lump in the winter.

Blanketing

The need and practicality of blanketing horses is a common question of horse owners. While there are many horses who live out their lives without ever being blanketed, blankets are advisable for many reasons.

The main function of blanketing is to keep the horse warm and dry when turned out in inclement weather. The horse is much more efficient than you would expect at maintaining his body temperature in cold weather and has managed to survive quite nicely in the wild without the benefit of man or his blankets. However, he accomplishes this only at the expense of burning tremendous amounts of body fat and even muscle tissue, and the horse that is constantly on turnout in cold weather without the benefit of a blanket will require much more feed than in milder weather (see Chapter 4, "Seasonal Care") to prevent a dramatic drop in condition.

Also, while the horse's coat is very effective in holding moisture on the surface, it is far from impervious. Horses who become soaked while on turnout are far more likely to have trouble regulating their body temperature and to experience a drop in their resistance to disease. (Getting wet or "catching a chill" cannot of itself cause a horse to get sick. However, the stress of trying to keep a stable body temperature under these conditions does weaken his resistance significantly.) These repeated exposures to wet conditions also increase the likelihood of the horse developing skin infections, as discussed in detail in Chapter 4, "Seasonal Care."

Blankets should consist of an outer water-repellent or -resistant layer with an underlying light sheet that can be easily thrown into the washing machine when it becomes dirty. Horses on constant turnout should be fitted with a heavy canvas blanket, with or without insulating material on the underside, which has straps that crosscross across the belly and straps for each hindleg. This arrangement helps to secure the blanket in place under turnout conditions, although in many circumstances even these may not be sufficient and you will need to add a surcingle or overgirth on top of the blankets for added security. The original design of these canvas blankets is sold as the "New Zealand Rug," and there are also several copies that work just as well. All are fairly expensive but should come with a guarantee not to rip. Horses who are turned out individually or in only small groups and are stabled for part of the day can probably get by with a specially treated, water-resistant, heavy cloth outer blanket if care is taken not to turn the horse out during heavy rain or snowstorms. The inner, washable layer can be a simple stable sheet of lightweight cotton or other cloth.

Blanketing is advisable in winterlike weather, even if a good shelter is provided, as horses will sometimes show remarkably poor judgment in getting in out of the bad weather, and a horse low on the pecking order may be kept out of shelters. The blanketing system described above, when properly applied, should stay in place even if the horse is not checked for several days. However, there are some horses who manage to destroy any blanket yet invented and others who will have the most elaborate system unhooked and the blankets around their ears or under their feet in no time at all. Still another problem when horses are turned out in a group is the occasional finding of a horse who seems to hate the sight of a blanket and will devote his time to destroying the blanketing of every horse in the herd. If you have one or more of these problems and cannot keep the horse blanketed, he can still be kept on turnout if care is taken to provide enough feed to meet his increased needs, if good shelter is available (preferably with more than one shed so that all may find a spot), if stabling is available for really terrible weather, and if arrangements can be made to provide good grooming. Even if these conditions cannot be met, the horse will survive the experience, but the problems of weight loss, illness, and skin disease can be expected.

Grooming

As a final note on general management, there is the subject of grooming. How often the horse is brushed, if at all, is more a matter of personal inclination than a necessity. It is advisable, however, to keep the fetlocks and back of the fetlocks trimmed close or even shaven to minimize the chances of dermatitis, "scratches," in this region. This condition is caused by infection of small breaks in the skin caused by plants, sharp grasses, dry twigs, and the like, and is made far worse when the hair is long and air does not circulate well. It is also wise to at least consider roaching the mane (shaving it off) if it is not going to be kept pulled short. Long manes have no use, are unnecessarily hot in summer, and once matted become far more unsightly and troublesome than a roached mane. A roached mane is also less likely to harbor ticks that could be carrying Lyme disease. It is also advisable to at least groom the horse regularly during the period the winter coat is being shed. Shedding out is often delayed in older horses and this sets the stage for bacterial or fungal infections often collectively referred to as "rain rot."

With "rain rot," large clumps of hair come out at the follicle, embedded in a crust, to leave open, weepy areas on the skin. The condition is very difficult to treat without clipping the horse. The treatment requires daily baths, preferably with Betadine or another iodine-based shampoo, and removal of all scabbing areas. In some cases it is also necessary to apply fungicide rinses to the coat, such as 5 tablespoons of Captan diluted in 1 gallon of water. Treatment often requires a minimum of ten days to begin to be effective and is best avoided entirely by close vigilance on horses with long coats.

HERD PSYCHOLOGY

Perhaps the greatest appeal of retiring a horse to pasture is the thought he will live out his days in a natural state. However, you may get more than you bargained for when your horse "goes native."

All horses develop an increased independence when turned out. In some, this is manifested as a total unwillingness to associate with humans that can have you chasing around a pasture for hours or bringing in the whole group before your horse can be caught. Also, if you come for your horse at the same time each day, he may take to always being at the most remote point in the field when you arrive. This results in some terrific exercise but is very frustrating to devoted owners who envision their faithful friend as being delighted by a visit.

There is some consolation to be had in realizing this behavior indicates the horse is adapting well and does indeed enjoy and prefer his new life. The horse that is too eager to be brought in may feed your ego but is probably very uncomfortable physically or socially (unless, of course, your arrival signals a meal). It is perfectly acceptable to bring food to catch a horse, but you should be aware that every other horse will be interested as well and you could find yourself in the middle of a battle. A

Older horses appreciate companions on turnout. From left to right: "Ronald McDonald Esquire," a 16-year-old Saddlebred gelding; "Tuesday's Blue Lady," a 19-year-old Anglo-Arabian mare; and "Marghabs Morning Star," a 28-year-old Arabian-Morgan cross gelding. Photograph by Lee Foley, Syracuse, New York.

better system would be to always carry a carrot or apple in your clothing. This will not attract the attention of the rest of the group although your horse will quickly learn to expect to find this reward. An added advantage is that it will be easier to actually catch the horse if he is focused on you rather than grabbing quick mouthfuls out of a bucket and dodging beyond your reach.

Alternately, maladjustment may be manifested as refusal to cooperate even after the horse is caught. A personality change like this is often seen in the horse at the bottom of the group pecking order and/or one that has not been accepted into a group. Whether the horse is redirecting his aggression at an easier target (you) or simply acting up out of extreme agitation is unclear. In any event, observation of his interactions while on pasture will probably show he is being ostracized or bullied, even prevented from eating and drinking in peace.

The dynamics of herd behavior are fascinating and have practical importance to your horse's welfare. An established herd will have a domi-

Twenty-year-old "Kharim" (white), owned by Elvia Gignoux, and 12-year-old "Rooster," owned by Peggy Kauffman, enjoying each other's company on one of their days off. Photograph by Sam Gignoux.

nant mare and possibly a dominant gelding as well. These horses are the first to eat and may chase away the others. If the field is large, the group will tend to follow the dominant horse of either sex, although mares will not attempt to force the group to move as a dominant gelding might.

Every other horse in the group also has a status, measured by how many of the herd will yield to him or her. The easiest time to assess a horse's rank is during feeding.

In addition to their individual status, the horses will tend to form groups or cliques with two to three others of similar rank. This is best observed when the herd is grazing as the cliques will drift apart at these times.

A newcomer almost always must undergo some rite of passage. Mares generally fare better, as the geldings of the group will rarely bother a mare and may actually try to add her to their group. The other mares, however, are often very aggressive to a newcomer and commonly will charge and bite. (The gallantry of geldings does not extend to protecting the new mare from a dominant mare's assault.) Geldings must compete for acceptance by both sexes and may have more trouble gaining admission to a clique. If there is another horse in the herd that was a recent addition, these two will usually pair off at least temporarily, particularly if both are geldings. Otherwise, the newcomer will simply assume a low profile and may be observed attaching himself to a small band and following their movements from a discrete distance.

Exceptions occur if the new addition has a particularly strong personality. Since mares are usually taken up by a band very easily, there may not be any problems until feeding time when the newcomer refuses to yield to a more senior mare and fighting results. An angered mare can do real damage and does not hesitate to kick or bite with little or no antecedent threatening behavior.

An aggressive, i.e., studdish, gelding will probably tangle with both sexes. The stronger males will assert themselves immediately upon entry into the field, often sizing up the situation with astonishing speed and seeking out the established dominant male. There is rarely physical contact between geldings unless the newcomer chooses to force the issue. He may instead decide to try his luck with the mares.

The stronger mares will deal with him directly, again using hooves and teeth liberally to make their position clear. In large groups, the established dominant male will tolerate this behavior to a certain extent but may step in when the newcomer tries to move in on his favorite mares. Otherwise, large groups will eventually reorganize, with the newcomer forming a band of mares for himself.

This can be harder to follow than a soap-opera plot line and really need not be a major concern unless your horse falls at either end of the aggression spectrum. The extremely assertive horse is in danger of injuries

"Butterscotch," a 30-year-old Shetland pony, is shown here munching happily on grass, neatly shovelled free of snow. He also has the important task of baby-sitting foals as they are weaned. Owned by Judy Sears, Cazenovia, New York.

from fighting during the first few days, while the meek will fare very poorly at feeding time and may continue to do so for an indefinite period. These problems tend to be worse in large groups than in those where only two or three horses are pastured together. In any case, it is wise to observe how the horse interacts with his new group both at feeding and while the herd is grazing. Fighting for superiority is self-limiting; however, the passive horse must be watched closely to be sure he is receiving enough feed and not subject to constant harassment. Even if a problem is noted, intervention will only slow resolution and should be avoided except in extreme cases.

16

Saying Good-bye

I If you have reached the point where your horse is being retired, chances are good you will be faced with the issue of euthanasia some where down the road.

No owner wishes to see his horse suffer; however, the decision to put a horse down is a difficult one, particularly if it must be based on the quality of life rather than a clear-cut catastrophe.

On a practical level, there are certain measures you should take to guarantee your horse will never have to suffer because you could not be located to give permission for euthanasia. To begin with, the parties caring for the horse should have a current and workable set of phone numbers, preferably for more than one family member. If you are going to be away, even for only a day, take as much care to see you can be reached about the horse as you would for your children.

It is advisable to designate someone to act in your behalf if you cannot be contacted. This should be a knowledgeable friend or trainer. You may also opt to give your veterinarian a signed permission for anesthesia or euthanasia in advance of a problem and allow him to do what he feels is best.

Discuss with your agent and/or veterinarian exactly what your wishes would be. For example, you might decide that surgery for a broken bone would not be worth the pain the horse would endure but if the problem was colic you would want the vet to try to save the horse, or vice versa.

In reality, it will be impossible to predict all eventualities and you may wish to decide on no surgery under any circumstances or only if there is an excellent chance the horse will recover to live out his life comfortably.

In the last analysis your agent will have to exercise his own judgment, and all involved must be comfortable with this. Do not put vague constraints on this person, such as, "If it's possible, try to wait until I get back...." Your agent must be free to act in the horse's best interest.

When designating an agent, it is best to put the arrangement in writing. This can save critical time if the veterinarian or hospital attending to the horse in the emergency does not know you, since they must be very careful to avoid an unauthorized euthanasia. The document need not be elaborate. The following is a sample.

I, _____ , authorize _____
to act in my absence regarding all emergency decisions on medical/surgical treatment or euthanasia for the horse
_____(name)_____ , tatoo_____ , a ____ - year-old,
_____(color)_____ , ____(Sex)_____ .

          Owner _____
          Witness _____
          Date _____

If you do go to the trouble of designating an agent, be sure to keep the document with the horse, e.g., in the barn office or your tack trunk, where it will be readily accessible.

If the horse is insured, the company will usually require notification prior to euthanasia or surgery. Attach the appropriate names and phone numbers of people to contact to your other emergency information and make sure everyone is aware of the situation in advance. Also, if you do make arrangements for an agent inform the insurance company of these details. An emergency is no time for lengthy explanations to the insurance company.

As a final practical consideration, give some thought to disposal of the body. Burying a horse is a major undertaking, and there may also be local regulations prohibiting this practice or dictating depth of burial. It is advisable to not only have a site reserved, but to plan in detail how the horse will be moved and what will be used to dig the hole.

Most people opt to have the body removed and disposed of by a renderer. These can be found in the yellow pages in most localities and there is no need to make prearrangements. Renderers are usually very good about arriving promptly. Most will also euthanize the horse for you (bullet to the brain) if you so wish and actually do a very neat and profes-

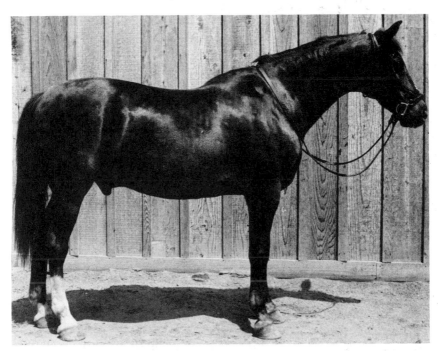

Owner Anita Sohus credits "good genes" for the health and longevity of her 30-year-old "Sam," who is reported to be half Tennessee Walker and the other half a mixture of Thoroughbred, Arabian, and Mustang!

sional job. However, there is nothing dignified in the sight of a horse being hoisted into a truck by chains, so you may want to arrange not to be present for this. It is not necessary to be on the premises when the renderer arrives, but someone should be present to give the authorization to euthanize the horse and remove the body, and you should identify this party to the renderer when you make the arrangements.

The moment will be over for the horse before he realizes anything is going on, so the decision of whether to remain for the proceedings is up to the individual owner. Most would prefer to say their last good-byes and then leave.

Accepting euthanasia in theory, and even providing for the eventuality, is miles away from the reality of it all. The fact remains that many, if not most, horses will not die of natural causes.

When the question arises suddenly, as with a severe colic or broken bone, owners often feel pressured, confused, and overwhelmed. These very understandable emotions may be intensified if the veterinarian involved is a stranger.

It is vitally important for the horse's sake that you remember the veterinarian has the horse's best interests in mind. No one enjoys destroying an animal or makes the recommendation lightly. Try to remain calm, listen carefully to the reasons euthanasia is being suggested, and ask questions until you understand. You could also ask for a second opinion if this request would not cause an inordinate delay. If you are having trouble reaching the decision, be guided by how much the horse is suffering and/or is likely to suffer.

I recall a Quarter Horse who was brought into New Bolton Center in the early stages of botulism poisoning. This disease causes a progressive paralysis with inability to move or stand, inability to swallow, and eventual paralysis of the respiratory muscles. Most horses panic and become unmanageable fairly early in the course of the disease.

This horse, however, was almost unbelievably intelligent, trusting, and cooperative. He conserved his energy and therefore was better able to help us when we periodically got him to his feet in a sling. He even had the sense to alternate the side he would go down on when he tired. The owners were several hours away from the hospital but were in regular phone contact and had been informed of the very poor prognosis in attempts to prepare them for the worst.

The horse held his own for forty-eight hours but then began to show the telltale changes in his breathing that signalled the paralysis was worsening and his lungs filling with fluid. Even in the short time he had been in the hospital everyone developed a strong bond of respect and admiration for this horse. He knew he was fighting for his life and also knew he was losing the battle.

The owners were contacted and asked to give permission for euthanasia. They were told that the disease progresses rapidly once the point of altered breathing is reached and that the horse would eventually suffocate. They were told the horse was dying, but despite this felt they could not possibly give permission until they saw him for themselves.

The following hours were pure hell for the horse and those caring for him. By the time his owners arrived, his once clear, expressive eyes were filled with panic, his mouth was blue, and he was covered with sweat and straw from struggling against his invisible attacker. Permission for euthanasia was given then, but instead of providing a peaceful, dignified release it was a struggle to wrestle him still long enough to infuse the drug that would finalize his defeat.

Every equine veterinarian has been faced with some variation of this dilemma where the owner is not present and hesitates to give permission for euthanasia. It is easy to become too involved in your own feelings of loss at the expense of the horse. The kindest and most difficult thing is to have the courage to say good-bye.

The famous Thoroughbred racehorse "Kelso" at the age of 27, appearing with his stablemate "Pate" for a final bow to his fans at the 1983 Jockey Club Gold Cup. Photograph by CARYN.

As horrible as these agonal scenes are, equally tragic are the horses condemned to a life with constant pain or disability. "Natural" deaths virtually never are a tranquil going to sleep on a full stomach, never to awaken. If the horse does not succumb to an acute catastrophe, such as colic or injury, he may linger for many months unable to obtain sufficient food, water, or shelter until malnutrition, dehydration, and weakness claim him.

No one wants to be guilty of such neglect, but the fact is that it is often very difficult to clearly see how much a horse has deteriorated when the downhill course is a slow one. It is also very difficult to reach a decision for euthanasia if your old friend is still functional at any level.

There are some reasonable steps you can take to avoid letting matters get out of hand. To begin, when you decide to retire the horse, make a list of all his problems such as lameness, respiratory disease, visual defects, and so forth. Next, ask your veterinarian to describe how the disease progresses, what to look for at each stage, and how the advancing disease will affect the horse's daily life. For example, when a horse is on turnout there are several telltale signs that he is losing the ability to function. Such horses are often isolated from others as they seek to avoid any chance of a confrontation from which they cannot defend themselves or flee. These horses are also the last to get feed or water, if they get it at all, and will hang back when the group is rounded up. They may also spend increasing amounts of time lying down. Eventually, coat quality and weight begin to drop off, sure signs the horse has been significantly stressed for quite some time.

Finally, decide in advance what your course of action will be. You may elect to euthanize a horse with eye problems when he first starts to bump into things, instead of waiting for a serious injury. With a lameness problem, you may draw the line when he has trouble competing for food, or with a heavey horse when even a walk to the water causes flaring of his nostrils and uncontrollable coughing. If you have trouble realistically evaluating the horse, ask the opinion of your veterinarian or any other knowledgeable person who does not see the horse as regularly as you do. Their perspective can be very helpful and they may give you an entirely different opinion on how well the horse is doing.

The use of functional guidelines may seem arbitrary, even trivial. However, all are symptomatic of a horse with severe problems adapting to the routine activities of daily living and correspond to an underlying physical compromise. If you understand the disease process and attempt to humanely and intelligently decide where to draw the line, you will have taken a major step toward assuring your horse's last days are truly enjoyable and peaceful.

Index

R